N-STINCTIVE

ROSIE TOMKINS

N-STINCTIVE

THE POWER OF
NATURAL INTELLIGENCE

Urbane
BUSINESS

urbanepublications.com

First published in Great Britain in 2020 by Urbane Publications Ltd,
Unit E3 The Premier Centre Abbey Park Romsey SO51 9DG
Copyright © Rosie Tomkins, 2020

A CIP catalogue record for this book is available from the British Library.

ISBN 978-1-912666-65-2
EBOOK 978-1-912666-66-9

Design and Typeset by Julie Martin
Cover by Julie Martin

Printed and bound by 4edge UK

urbanepublications.com

For Dr Alison Winch, thought leader and game changer. How I wish we could have walked shoulder-to-shoulder along this path for a little while longer.

TESTIMONIALS

"This is a fantastic book in many different ways. It widened my view about leadership and I love the framework used to introduce Natural Intelligence. It is an extremely engaging read with powerful stories and examples, which for me validated that leadership is about connecting in a transformational way with those people we serve as well as those we need to be leading. The author's authenticity shines through the entire book. Congratulations Rosie."

Pam Frost, previously Co-Director of Education, National Health Service, United Kingdom

"The concept of animal behaviour applied to leadership is inspiring and the author's demonstrated expertise is powerful. The specific examples bring the concepts to life and establish a personal connection with the reader."

Graham Miller, Partner, Clarke Mclean Financial, United Kingdom

"Lovely, inspiring and well written. Eminently readable. Great sincerity, authenticity and readability. I think it will be a hit."

Robin Teoh, Doctor of Medicine, United Kingdom

"This book touched my heart. It comes from the head and the heart, together, to show leadership in a more humble way. It is a new type of business book that opens you up to new ways of being. It can give you a renewed confidence and sense of purpose in yourself and in any role in any organisation. It reminds us that our natural intelligence is valued and should be allowed to flourish, alongside all our intelligences; to be free to be that liberated leader without fear; to be able to bring your best game to the table. As Rosie's beautifully written book says, "We are animals and we have everything we need to survive built into our DNA."

Paula Tully, previously Vice President Europe, Pfizer Biopharmaceutical UK, part of Escentia Ltd

"This book presents a unique, fun and innovative perspective about leadership. I am very familiar with the topic of Instinctual Intelligence and I really like the anecdotes about the different types of animals – who instinctually follow their inner knowing and stay congruent and balanced – and I appreciate how this relates to self and organizational leadership. In our modern age, we humans have become disconnected from ourselves and with nature and this book reminds us that we would be better off if we can find ways of tapping into and trusting our natural intelligence."

Lissa Pohl Head of Leadership at Kentucky University, United States of America

"What an inspiration! I love that we can become better leaders by understanding our animal selves through the natural world."

Chris Baréz-Brown, Motivator, Founder of Upping Your Elvis and author of four books

MESSAGE FROM THE LATE DAVID SHEPHERD

British Artist and Conservationist

"Rosie's work is thought-provoking and powerful. It has the courage to proclaim and remind us all of a simple, yet profound message; that despite man's sophistication we are still part of the herd.

As with all animals in the wild, leadership relies on Natural Intelligence and every leader of self, teams, organisations, institutions, or businesses will benefit from engaging with Rosie's words.

What we have always known and been shown from the animal kingdom is brought to life in a unique, accessible and vital way."

CONTENTS

FOREWORD

Rosie Tomkins has a zest for life and a passion for business. She is a force of nature with a big heart. She is bold. She cares. The combination is powerful. She changes lives.

Rosie understands power; how to use it and connect with it; and she empowers leaders to access more of their own. Power is an essential ingredient in today's volatile and competitive business world. Rosie also understands the power of horses and nature, which she translates into her conversations with visionary business leaders. As a previous founder and managing director of a lifestyle company, which she successfully sold to a dynamic PLC, Rosie spots an opportunity and moves fast. Now with her latest offer, N-stinctive, she integrates her deep knowledge and wisdom of leading people together with running businesses and having a family. She combines these skills with her years of experience as a competitive polo player and delivers unique training sessions for global thought leaders in equine leadership and elite performance.

Rosie is a consummate business woman and has a keen appetite for 'better.' Her work at N-stinctive truly provokes and inspires other people to do 'better' and gain tangible breakthrough results. Eternally curious, she started investigating patterns in equine behaviour and human communication. She transformed her research into impactful and practical exercises enabling horses to assist leadership teams and individual leaders to be 'better' leaders in their businesses and in their personal lives. She sports an impressive client list and in this intelligent book, Rosie once again takes the reins and leads us down a practical path to instinctive, natural leadership.

She learned her mantra from working with horses and understanding their Natural Intelligence.

Do I feel safe?

Do I trust you?

Who is leading right now?

These words speak volumes. As relevant in the boardroom as they are in a paddock. Her book asks us to consider: our positioning; our best place to succeed; our pace; the speed at which we achieve things; and how to use all of ourselves. Especially our own instinctive responses to whatever hurdles business and life bring our way. Jump into the book when you are ready, but jump!

MICHELE SEYMOUR, FOUNDER, BALANCE MATTERS

AN IDEA WHOSE TIME HAS COME!

NOT ANOTHER BUSINESS BOOK I hear you saying. Well, this time it is a business book you can read in half-a-day and apply immediately to your working environment.

It is simple, memorable and uplifting.

After more than 30 years of consultancy, building successful businesses, coaching, training hundreds of young leaders and working with specialist groups – including Olympic sports teams – I wanted to challenge many of the common assumptions and traits of business books.

Why are many of the outstanding business books linked with sport? As a life-long lover of all sport I enjoy reading all the sporting metaphors. However, I have started to challenge the exclusivity of sport. I am aware that all the values of courage, discipline, teamwork, tenacity, skill, commitment, endurance etc. have inspirational meaning for all of us. Yet, most sports require us to be young and fit and that one individual or team wins; the rest lose. It can be brutal, dangerous, and promote an adapt-or-die mentality, be goal-oriented, and push an all or nothing culture. Loyalties are often to contracts or sponsorship; people, especially managers, are disposable. Spectators have zero tolerance for mistakes or weakness and this tribal mentality can be barbaric at times. Overall it is a culture with a short lifespan, where ecstasy can quickly become despair.

In this book, I am advocating a shift from sports metaphors to nature metaphors, where anything is possible. Where age, gender, diversity or cash do not prejudice a successful outcome. Where everyone can be inspired, can fit in – an inclusive and collaborative and gentler way of being successful. Not another formula exclusively for winning, being happy or successful. Not another brilliant business strategy to develop, simply a return to what animals have been naturally reflecting for thousands of years: purpose; adaption; resilience; pressure; responsibility; wisdom; ritual; collaboration; and buckets of inspiration.

We seem to be constantly emphasising that people are different to animals. However, we are simply a different species. Let's move away from the illusion of separation.

But why am I advocating this approach, and what are my qualifications for doing so? For the last 10 years I've worked internationally pioneering a unique leadership development and coaching technique called *NQ instinctive intelligence*. This compassionate and cutting edge approach is known as equine facilitated leadership and involves work with horses. The horses allow us to get out of our heads and literally come to our senses. This creates greater opportunities to explore situations in a completely different way, discover insights and bring about exceptional learning. Horses provide a natural leadership simulator that is impossible to achieve in a classroom-based learning situation. They are experts in non-verbal communication and sentient learning. Horses don't have an agenda. They don't care what car you drive, how much money you have in the bank or how important you are. There is no ego at play and you cannot fake the outcome which means that an honest conversation has space to emerge. The horses simply reflect our strength of character, our heart, our internal incongruence and our self-limiting beliefs and perception. They allow people to explore and embody the insights that create lasting transformation, preparing individuals and teams to meet their biggest challenges.

We are not in nature ... we are nature!

LEADERSHIP SIMULATOR

Would you step onto an aircraft if you knew the pilot had only read a book about flying? No, you put your life in their hands because you know they have spent hundreds of hours in a flight simulator. They are experts at what they do, because they know what it feels like to fly an aircraft through an electric storm. They know how it feels when they lose a tyre on take-off. They know how it feels to land a jumbo jet in a fierce crosswind. Most of all, you need to feel that they have confidence in their own ability to cope under pressure, whatever happens.

Why then would you expect any leader not to go through the same rigorous training? And how can this all be taught in the classroom, or from models, or books, or online? In business we are obsessed with technique. Does technique alone make you a safe pilot? How can we embody and feel a deep trust that we have all that we need, from reading a business manual or completing a course online?

I believe we need a Leadership Simulator, where we can hone our skills, make our mistakes without catastrophic results, celebrate our innate abilities and those of our teams, and initiate new ways and ideas without suppression. Memories are stored in the muscles. They are literally embodied. Imagine a leadership simulator that combines the skills and techniques of the leading thought strategies with a deep understanding of your own personal physiology. And can assess the impact stress and pressure have on your decision-making capabilities and general wellbeing.

I believe this leadership simulator has to be outside the classroom, it has to be experiential, and it has to include the 'N Factor' – the nature factor – working alongside other living beings. Imagine getting immediate feedback in a non-judgemental way from another living thing that has no vested interest. It would be incredibly valuable.

This Leadership Simulator has to take you outside your comfort zone and challenge your deeply held beliefs in a unique way that will make you stronger and more confident in your own ability. It makes sense to feel leadership and embody it in a safe environment, before you experience the volatile, uncertain, complex and ambiguous world of business and life. Only then can you successfully navigate this fast-moving world that we all live in.

I also believe that in today's world there is too much mindless data, too much evidence-based policies, too much management talk, committees, groupthink etc. and that there is not enough natural instinct brought into the decision-making process.

For some people instinct is a dirty word, it conjures up a

rampaging survival of the fittest ethos. However, in this book I will provide evidence that animals are far more collaborative in their natural habitat than we give them credit for, in fact they often use rotational leadership, for example the flight formation of wild geese, to shoulder the burden of fatigue, which makes them more efficient as a group or a team. We can learn a lot from the collective and collaboratives ways animals in the wild support each other, during times of abundance as well as scarcity.

Study the grid below and ask yourself the questions that follow.

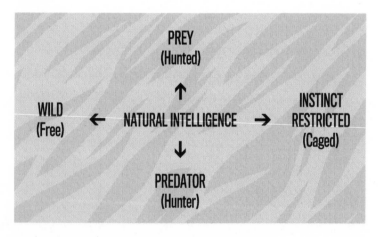

Where am I on this grid right now?

Is instinct core to my important life decisions?

How relevant is my 'nature factor?' Could I choose healthier options/habits for the future?

This book will introduce you to the concept of Natural Intelligence. From my work over the past 30 years running training within many corporate and small business organisations, I have come to the realisation that something very important is missing from our leadership and training programs and I call this missing ingredient Natural Intelligence. (NQ)

NATURAL INTELLIGENCE

Natural intelligence is the positive use of your instincts, insights and perceptions. As noted by Mark H. McComack in his book What they don't teach you at Harvard Business School , "Executives who have a finely tuned people sense and awareness of how to apply this, invariably take the edge in any situation." They know that Natural Intelligence requires you to open to the senses exactly like a wild animal, picking up invaluable information by watching closely, listening, interpreting signals, whether conscious or unconscious, recognising boundaries, spotting defensive stubborn or aggressive patterns, gaining knowledge about comfort zones – reading behind the eyes. All of which translates into dramatically improved and well-honed interpersonal skills.

There is no disputing the fact that many people already use natural intelligence every day and yet it is not always acknowledged on CVs or given the credit it deserves. Take the caring professions as an example. Many of us have experienced kindness and support at a vulnerable time from a person who instinctively knew what was appropriate for our wellbeing. Sometimes this ability is totally natural, sometimes it can be learnt or enhanced. However it is accumulated, this valuable attribute needs to be polished, protected and recognised in every genre of life.

I believe that this natural intelligence needs to be at the core of all awareness training, especially in universities, training institutes and business schools. It is a way of balancing the heady methodologies with something just as important in leadership – belief in self – which animals demonstrate every day.

My definition of leadership is a dynamic combination of self-awareness, multiple intelligences and highly developed interpersonal skills. At the moment my observation of leadership training is that it is a three-legged stool, but actually it needs to be a four-legged chair.

All of the intelligences IQ (Intelligence Quotient) + EQ (Emotional Quotient) + SQ (Spiritual Quotient) + NQ (Natural Intelligence) need to be valued equally. This formula will then provide us with memorable – mental and physical – anchors to support us as leaders when the world becomes increasingly complex so we can stay grounded and resolute.

There is a huge chasm between theory and practice; between awareness and action; and between what we know and what we do.

SCRATCH THE SURFACE AND WE ARE ALL ANIMALS

No matter how sophisticated, educated and advanced the human race has become we still, bleed, fight, mate, protect our young, burp, pass wind, scratch our noses, and our behinds! We still struggle to control our natural biology. The pheromones still scream to be satisfied. We cannot suppress fear, passion and aggression, no matter how hard we try.

Many experts say that communication is roughly 90% non-verbal and 10% verbal, yet we seem so limited in our awareness of the non-verbal dialogue, the predominant language of most species.

No matter how prestigious our position in life and how famous, how credible, how royal, how rich, how talented how intelligent and how enlightened we are, our limbic brain is still naturally hardwired to our innate animal responses. Perhaps if we were encouraged to use our peripheral vision and all our combined natural senses more often we could influence the world from a more grounded perspective?

OFF-TRACK

Due to the amazing technological advances the world over, our way of living has been disrupted. This is inevitably going to affect our younger generation and the leaders of tomorrow. We are in danger of disconnecting from our own natural and intuitive knowledge, and a reliance on 'expert advice' is ever present in all aspects of our life and career. These experts tell us what to eat, how to decorate our homes and how to bring up our children ... and the list goes on. We have leadership models or archetypes, we follow rules and often observe constraints that no longer serve us, we look to medical technology to heal us and keep us healthy and we take courses on how to manage people. Are we losing our initiative and our natural flair? Are we losing faith in our own judgement?

If we were to tap into the more than 400,000 years of evolution installed in our biology, we would find that our ancestors had to take control of complex scenarios and ever-present threats to stay alive. This is still embedded in our DNA. We simply need to know how to access it. Our ancestors made life-saving decisions every day. They knew instinctively what to do. There were no experts to ask, no books to read, no maps to follow, no internet search engines. They had to trust everything they needed was already within themselves and they were right!

This book will take a look at nature in the raw to see what valuable lessons we can utilise to cut through today's complexities. It will provide you with memorable anchors that will give you an edge in almost any situation you encounter throughout your life.

THIS BOOK IS FOR YOU IF YOU ARE A ...

- Change maker
- Thought leader
- Business leader
- Team member
- Collaborator
- Individual
- High achiever
- Early adopter
- Pioneer
- New thinker
- Positive influencer

THIS BOOK WILL INSPIRE YOU IF YOU ARE ...

- Looking for something uplifting and thought provoking in the leadership arena

- Tired of the existing leadership material

- Prepared for the honest conversation

- Wanting to be nourished

- Questioning the status quo

- Wanting to be aligned with your purpose

- Hoping to make a difference

- Looking for new answers

- Responsible for other people

- Investing in yourself and other people

HOW TO USE THIS BOOK

All the chapters of this book are interwoven to position you as a liberated leader. Throughout this book, there will be interludes where I insert true client stories, together with personal stories about my life. Where necessary, names have been changed to protect identity.

Even the simplest stories can lead to profound insights for both teams and leaders. By understanding how all the intelligences (IQ, EQ, SQ, NQ) link together, we can create more harmony in business and less stress and competition.

The cited quotations from international change makers and world leaders, are chapter referenced at the back of the book.

The quotations in bold are my messages for you; to help you on your journey to being a liberated leader, using your Natural Intelligence for an improved world future.

CHAPTER 1

SPORT OF KINGS

THIS IS A TRUE STORY about a young boy I have known for many years. His name is Jack and this is his story.

JACK'S STORY

Jack was born in Italy, the son of an Italian show jumper and a British groom. Jack didn't spend much time with his father and at an early age returned to England with his mother. They didn't have much money nor many possessions, but his mother created a life for them both; a life that was always turbulent and often precarious. She earned her living in jobs associated with hunting and on working farms. The work was hard and the hours long.

Young Jack was small, Italian, dyslexic and partially blind in one eye and although he felt at peace in the countryside, he hated school and whenever possible absconded. He was always found shadowing the local gamekeeper, or beating for the local pheasant shoots. Warmth, love and support were not part of his life, but he survived. When his mother landed a job at a polo club, Jack whizzed around on his bike playing bicycle polo, while his more fortunate contemporaries played on ponies.

Despite his rough start in life, there was always something special about Jack. He had a quiet confidence in his ability to look after himself; he had no pretensions and no fear of others people or their expectations. At school he told the girls that one day he was going to be rich and famous by travelling the world playing international polo. Oh, how they laughed!

Jack's first break came when he was lent a small polo pony. Watching him ride this pony was amazing; a visual joy. With not one riding lesson in his life Jack worked his magic on his horse and on the game. His skill and ability were extraordinary. His raw natural talent shone through and 'the David Beckham of Polo' was launched.

But his luck didn't last. In another twist of fate, his mother married a wealthy landowner. With this partnership came a stepbrother who was rich, tall and wanted to play polo. He was given everything Jack wasn't – expensive ponies, heaps of support and plenty of encouragement. This boy had everything that was missing in Jack's life. It wasn't long before Jack's hard-earned ways clashed with his new lifestyle and he was told to pack his bags and make a new life elsewhere.

It was a tough life as a polo groom, but at only 17 years old Jack had one thing going for him – he believed in himself, a belief that nothing could diminish. Jack knew who he was and what he was capable of. He would not live someone else's life or conform to other people's values or expectations. And as often happens in life, the tables started to turn for Jack.

One day, he received a telephone call; he was offered a last-minute chance to fill in for a rider at a polo tournament. Jack's natural talent for riding and for polo was noticed and he started to compete regularly at the polo club tournaments. It was during an event at the prestigious Cowdray Park, playing in the final match, that he was spotted by the England squad. Jack was plucked from obscurity to play for the England polo team!

Now you could say that it was his natural talent which gave him this opportunity, and in some ways you would be right. It is true he was blessed with superb hand-eye coordination and a natural ability to ride. But I truly believe his hard upbringing had given him something many of us have lost. Jack knew how to access his natural intelligence – his authentic self – and his unique internal compass.

He is who he is, he does not follow the herd. He is true to himself always.

I was privileged to watch Jack play in his first match for the Young England Team. This is the sport of kings and exactly like motor racing, you need money to be part of its privileged world, which includes: expensive trimmings; thoroughbred horses; glitzy events; gleaming leather; and an entourage of helpers. To witness how Jack survived in this world was unforgettable. He ate his cornflakes out of the back of his beaten up car; he had no money to pay for grooms; his mother rushed around helping him with his forgotten polo sticks; his girlfriend sorted out the horses; and Jack – in the middle of all this chaos – was totally unfazed; with his quietly confident and unassuming manner he remained steady throughout.

Watching him ride out onto the polo ground in his England team shirt and score the first two goals was truly momentous; but there was always more to Jack. The highlight was seeing him stop to help an opponent remount after a fall. It was a gesture of true sportsmanship that doesn't often happen in polo, especially in an important match. His critics gave him abuse for wasting time; but the crowd gave him a standing ovation. They genuinely admired a man who could make such a gesture of compassion at one of the most important moments of his career.

He now travels the world playing international polo; exactly as he always said he would!

But what has this story got to do with Natural Intelligence?

This story introduces the central theme of this book;

how to strengthen your innate leadership skills.

We all know how important it is to lead yourself before you can lead other people, before you can lead organizations and before you can lead in the world.

Jack's story demonstrates his intuitive natural abilities. His essence and life force are there for everyone to see – his belief in himself, his resilience, his courage, his vision, his focus. He is naturally demonstrating liberated leadership.

His understanding of his own personal values served him well, but will it be enough to sustain him through the complex and challenging times in which we all live?

Of course – the more he trusts in his own judgement, the more he will thrive. However, that does not mean he will float through life without disasters and heartache and that he will not benefit from some help along the way. Animals everywhere need help to survive in this new VUKA – volatile, uncertain, complex, ambiguous – world man has created.

STRESS AND SUCCESS

We talk about stress reduction and success all the time in business. Stress seems to go hand in hand with leadership, wouldn't you say?

It is undisputable that stress has become epidemic in proportions. According to the Huffington Post, our young people are more stressed than ever: one in four students are suffering from a diagnosable illness; the average age for depression is 14½ years old; and there is now a disorder called TBD, Too Busy Disorder!

Stress in the wild is a necessary way of being for most prey animals. They are continually under pressure from predators and are on high alert most of their lives. We are all aware of their coping mechanism of fight, flight or freeze. Yet, if you view any wildlife scene after a hunt you'll see the zebras walk side by side with the lions and the wildebeest strut peacefully alongside the hyenas, mere feet away from the carnage of a kill; all their collective energy dissipated very quickly.

This is what I call 'lion graze', mentally focusing on the energy not the threat. They do not stay in a stressed mode longer than is needed. However, in the human population we are in flight and fight mode continually, we seem to be constantly worrying or fearful that something will go wrong and we are on high alert the majority of the time.

How exhausting is that? What has happened to freeze?

Or lion graze?

Imagine a hare crouching stock still and low to the ground, its life force barely perceptible. Often the slightest movement is the difference between life and death; or being seen or not seen. This is freeze mode and animals are the experts in energetic awareness. If there is no movement or energy transmitted, they are often not picked off by prey. I often play a trick on my dog when I want to be alone. Although he can see me through the window, if I don't move he cannot detect my presence. So, he moves off to find someone or something more interesting. If the hare survives, it slowly emerges from its trance like state, shakes, rolls and literally jumps for joy; all stress hormones quickly dissipated.

When did you last jump for joy?

What is the currency for success? According to Robert Holden the modern formula for work success appears to be:

Human Success = greater speed + fewer resources + constant uncertainty + competition

We are literally killing ourselves in the name of success.

In the wild, what does the formula for success look like?

Animal Success = short burst of speed + abundant resources + collaboration + rest and recovery

In fact, the human formula for success needs simply to be as follows:

IQ + EQ +SQ + NQ (Natural Intelligence) = Success

These multiple intelligences, when applied together in the decision-making process, will give a more balanced outcome. The outcome will be a life well lived, aligned to your purpose, embracing what you love. I believe that with all these components equally valued, you can truly fulfil your potential; achieving success, with a huge reduction in stress.

COURSED OUT!

This is the bane of so many employees.

What is it about professional courses? Nowadays, whenever you mention courses, there is a collective sigh. Especially in large organisations where they have a budget for training and requirements that employees must tick the boxes on a regular basis. Most organisations continue to rely on 'death by PowerPoint' in presentations. The truth is that no matter how inspiring the facilitator or material is, it is difficult to sustain or remember the content for more than two or three days after completing the course.

Even more demotivating can be the tools used to measure employee performance in most large organisations. The personal appraisal; the 360-degree feedback process; the KPIs (key performance indicators).

As Chris Barez-Brown neatly puts it, "I can only assume that they are designed to extinguish all hope and make staff thoroughly miserable about the work they do."

Natural Intelligence appeals to individuals who are coursed out! They may be questioning their own judgement and be sick of not being able to express themselves fully. They are probably feeling generally uninspired, unappreciated and jaded. They may feel as if they are on a hamster wheel with no true authenticity.

Or they may be disappointed with their career prospects and are losing confidence in their own ability and are tired of faking it. Most of all, they are looking for something that will reinvigorate their outlook.

Animals don't read self-help books and they don't go on courses!

And yet, it is rare to see dejection and hopelessness in the animal kingdom.

REAL PEOPLE, REAL LEARNING

I am fortunate because my work sometimes involves elite sportsmen and women, often when they are looking for marginal gain. On this occasion, a team was performing really well on the world circuit, but was experiencing interpersonal challenges, which was causing frustration and damaging the respect that is so important for performance.

The team's star player was a superstar on the pitch, stepping at speed into turbulent deep waters. Courageous, not limited by boundaries, happy to be upfront and personal, a forward-moving mountain of pure muscle, great to have next to you when the territory is tough, energy at 101 per cent. Off the pitch he was a major hazard in nearly all social situations; too bold, too pushy, in your face, unaware of personal boundaries, overstepping the mark. Always in the papers, volatile and mouthy, with no conscious recognition of his impact on other people.

The brief was to cement the trust, respect and diverse leadership styles of all team members both on and off the pitch, without destroying the unique essence or value that each player contributes.

So, it was with huge curiosity that I introduced this star player to the horses. Firstly, we worked through several exercises to build rapport, boundaries, trust and a safe environment.

Secondly, we moved on to the real challenges of the day.

I asked each individual to partner with a horse of their choice. It was unsurprising that this star player chose the alpha male in the group. A magnificent horse with immense presence and athleticism. The delegates were asked to complete a challenge, which I call Equine Billiards.

It involves imagining the paddock as a billiard table and manoeuvring the horses into a pocket on the table without touching them, purely by using one's own personal leadership style and energy.

Immediately, the horses picked up on this individual's energy and moved as far away from him as possible, which was to the far side of the paddock. There, the horses stayed until the man approached them again with a powerful presence bordering on intimidation. Trapped against the paddock rails, one of the horses was cornered and becoming anxious. Immediately, I stopped the challenge because there was a danger of triggering a flight or fight response. However, there was enough information demonstrated already by this situation to have a powerful debrief.

What did you notice?

Why did that happen?

Where else does this happen in your life?

What learning can you take away and apply immediately?

In a very natural way, the horses had acted as a living metaphor, which allowed a non-emotive conversation around how our behaviour can impact other people.

How we can unintentionally cause fear, by rushing through boundaries. How we can celebrate this energy and direct combative behaviour on the sports field, but maybe tone it down when away from it. Being able to stop, check in and ask oneself, what is appropriate right now?

The team Captain's feedback included the following.

"The key aspect that came out of the experience was that by working as a team we could build confidence and belief. It totally connects you with your work colleagues. Once you really know yourself, you can move on to other people too and you can really see and feel how they operate. It takes a while to understand our own individual Natural Intelligence, but working with the horses reconnects you with doing what you feel is right and believing in it; the absolute key to a successful team."

INSTINCTIVE INSIGHTS

- Understanding the power of YOU.
- Celebrating personal power and diversity.

- Understanding the difference between intention and making something actually happen.

- Instinctively to know, what's appropriate right now?

- Understanding your unique personal leadership style.

- Deep learning in a safe environment.

- Building strong future relationships based on respect.

"Security does not exist in nature, nor do the children of men as a whole experience it."

HELEN KELLER

Do you truly know your personal leadership impact?

CHAPTER TWO

BORN FREE

WHEN WE TALK ABOUT LEADERSHIP, we often refer to the giants such as Nelson Mandela, Martin Luther King, Mother Teresa, and many more. Their contribution to our world has been awe-inspiring; their legacy will live forever. However, for the average person these examples of exceptional leadership can be a stretch too far and may have the opposite effect; possibly even be demotivating.

"How can I reach those heights? I am not destined to be another great human being, so why am I bothering to try?"

In this chapter, I want to celebrate the fact that we are all born free. We are all born to be who we want to be. And I want to honour those priceless leadership moments that happen every day, in our lives and in the lives of the creatures around us.

My motivation for this chapter comes from the words of David Shepherd, wildlife expert and champion of all things wild. He used to start all his talks with this statement:

"You can build another Taj Mahal or St Paul's cathedral, but you can never build another tiger."

DAVID SHEPHERD

How true is that? I would go further and say; "You can build the highest tower in the world … but you can't build another you!" We cannot possibly see what lies ahead, only trust that our destiny will emerge, maybe at a much later date than we envisaged. Life is full of surprises.

"Two caterpillars were sitting on a leaf when a butterfly passed overhead. One caterpillar said to the other, 'You'd never get me up in one of those things.'"

BILLY CONNOLLY

Consider that in the wild a giraffe gives birth standing up. The baby falls between eight to ten feet onto the ground, normally landing on its back. Like a newborn it is immediately vulnerable to prey and many predators love giraffe meat. Instinctively, the mother knows she needs to encourage that baby up onto its feet as soon as possible. And although it seems barbaric to us, she kicks the baby giraffe hard, which stimulates the new born to struggle up onto its feet. This usually happens several times because their wobbly legs strengthen each time and the baby giraffe will be standing within an hour. The mother giraffe has bestowed the gift of life and she is conditioned to perform a lifesaving manoeuvre; however harsh it looks to us.

The giraffe baby is born free, but the struggle to survive begins immediately. All animals are born free. However, all wild animals are born with a genetic purpose that is hard-wired into their DNA. They have little choice about what they can become; a dog cannot become a zebra.

We as human animals, are also born free and our lives can be very difficult from an early age and sometimes throughout our entire existence. Many people are born into the most impoverished and violent scenarios. Sometimes, we don't have someone who will help us to get up when we fall, sometimes it is easier to stay down. However, we all have the freedom to choose our individual mindset.

Consider the famous message from Victor Frankl, from his renowned book, *Man's Search for Meaning*:

"Everything can be taken from a man but one thing - the last of the human freedoms - to choose one's attitude in any given set of circumstances, to choose one's own way."

VIKTOR FRANKL

We also have many tools and skills that can help us navigate choppy waters and make the right choices. Our ability to make choices and to pause before executing a decision differentiates us from other species. By being human we definitely have more options and maybe more freedom at our disposal. We have the ability to look at the circumstances or event objectively and pause to consider the desired outcome before we choose our response.

The giraffe has the natural instinct to help its young one to survive.

What does your natural instinct tell you right now about your survival?

With this amazing freedom what does man choose to create?

THE PARADOX OF OUR AGE

"We have bigger houses but smaller families.

More conveniences but less time.

We have more degrees but less sense.

More knowledge but less judgement.

More experts but more problems.

More medicines but less healthiness.

We've been all the way to the moon and back, but have trouble crossing the street to meet the new neighbour.

We build more computers, to hold more information, to produce more copies than ever, but have less communication.

We have become long on quantity but short on quality.

These are times of fast food but slow digestion.

Tall man but short character.

Steep profits but shallow relationships.

It's a time, when there is much in the window but nothing in the room."

THE 14TH DALAI LAMA

Remember no-one is going to make it happen for you – that is your job! It is our individual job to find our creativity; we are born free to choose our own creativity.

There are many 'experts' trying to tell us how to live our lives. What colour you should paint your house; how to bring up your children; what to eat; and how to run your own business, etc. Most of these questions you already know the answer to. We have simply lost confidence in our own natural judgement. There is no shortcut to being an expert on ourselves; we simply need to put in the work. And when I mean work, I mean knowing ourselves and becoming an expert in knowing ourselves.

Watching and observing animals in the wild is the first step in this process.

VALUE INDICATOR

As we know in business, the first question we tend to ask is, why have we started this business? Or why do I want to work with this organisation? What are we trying to achieve? How are we going to deliver the product or service?

Prioritising the values of the organisation is also a fundamental requirement in business and in an ideal world, the values of the business are aligned with the personal values of the employees.

How do you find these true values?

Well, one way to find your true values is to watch your own reaction in situations. When you feel any excessive emotion whether it be tears, anger or fear, it is an indicator of a value that is not being protected or is being abused or walked over.

Values are indicators of where you should be putting your energy. If you are not living your values on a day-to-day basis, you are not living on purpose and you are going to be faking it in some way.

Animals do not have the ability to fake it. They live a life congruent with their purpose.

"Do not piggy-back on someone else's wisdom."

ROBERT HOLDEN

REAL PEOPLE, REAL LEARNING

I want to share with you a true, personal story, which demonstrates a real example of leadership at its finest with someone who is living completely aligned with their own personal values.

It was one of those winter days when everything conspired to make me late for work: the children lost shoes; the cat had deposited a headless mouse on the doorstep; and I couldn't find the de-icer for the car windscreen. Eventually, I made it into the office and began to plough my way through a deluge of paperwork. My mind was bombarded with conflicting thoughts and I was struggling to see a clear path through my own personal jungle. After having sold my business successfully a few months beforehand, for some reason I was putting myself under pressure to build another enterprise and return to the cut and thrust of the entrepreneurial arena once again. But my heart wasn't in it and I was feeling battered, battle-worn and jaded. The day itself was uneventful and I left in time to arrive at a course on Neuro Linguistic Programming (NLP) that I had booked some time before.

The course time had been written clearly in my diary as 6-9pm and I was pleased when I arrived at 5.40pm. Time enough for a coffee and sandwich and perhaps a glimpse of the daily papers, I thought. What pleasure, an evening of watching, learning and listening, but most of all, an evening of being anonymous.

I arrived at the venue and was frustrated to see that although the course was scheduled to start at 6pm, the room was filled with people and many were already writing notes with the facilitator in full swing on the platform. How annoying! I managed to grab my coffee and although the door was shut, I proceeded to enter and sit down at a seat at the back. Everybody's heads swung round in unison and looked surprised to see me there. I interpreted this move as a judgement that I was five minutes late, so glared back in defiance.

The facilitator welcomed me with a friendly smile.

"How nice to see you," she said. "You have arrived at the right time because we are doing a session on heroes. I was wondering if you had a story in your life you remember that had a powerful hold on you and a relevance to your business?"

I nodded and to my horror she invited me to join her on the platform. She quickly drew the story out of me, it was the famous story of Androcles and The Lion, a well-known legend or fable that had stayed with me since my childhood:

A slave named Androcles once escaped from his master and fled to the forest. As he was wandering about, there he came upon a lion lying down moaning and groaning. At first, he turned to flee, but finding that the lion did not pursue him, he turned back and went up to him. As he came near, the lion put out his paw, which was all swollen and bleeding and Androcles found that a huge thorn had pierced it and was causing all the pain. He pulled out the thorn and bound up the paw of the lion, who was soon able to rise and lick the hand of Androcles like a dog. Then the lion took Androcles to his cave and every day used to bring him meat to nourish him.

But shortly afterwards, both Androcles and the lion were captured and the slave was sentenced to be thrown to the lion after the latter had been kept without food for several days. The Emperor and all his court came to see the spectacle and Androcles was led out into the middle of the arena. Soon the lion was let loose from his den and bounded roaring towards his victim.

But as soon as he came near to Androcles he recognised his friend and fawned upon him and licked his hands like a friendly dog. The Emperor, surprised at this, summoned Androcles to him who told him the whole story. Whereupon the slave was pardoned and freed and the lion let loose to his native forest.

Then the coaching began.

"What relevance has this story to your situation right now?"

"Well, I feel like I am in the lion's den, back in the cut and thrust of corporate life, with spectators watching my every move, waiting for me to fail and fall."

"Which character do you identify with and why?"

"I believe I am Androcles back in the fight."

"What do you think the story is telling you?"

"What do you feel is significant for you in the future?"

"How will you look at your life differently?"

As I answered these questions, the reality of my situation started to change, I saw a new perspective, something I had not considered before. Maybe, I was not Androcles, maybe I was the lion. I can choose to fight or not. How many times did Androcles and the lion go into the amphitheatre? The slow dawning came to me – it was only once before they were set free!

This quick-fire demonstration took approximately 20 minutes. Amazingly, the load that I been carrying in my life at that time was taken away; I felt released from a very heavy burden. The whole room applauded the short coaching session and laughed at my shocked expression when the facilitator thanked me for joining her 20 minutes before the end the course. The course had started at 12pm and was due to wrap up at 6pm. I was 5 hours 40 minutes late!

INSTINCTIVE INSIGHTS

I will never forget the generosity and the display of incredible leadership ability that I had witnessed that day. For this facilitator to seize the moment and create a learning opportunity out of it for her group was magnificent. She demonstrated all the required attributes of a powerful leader:

- Lack of surprise, when I catapulted into the room.

- Open to outcome, she had no agenda.

- Instinctive decision making that there could be a powerful learning behind the interruption.

- Complete mastery in asking the right questions.

- Concluding the day with warmth and a powerful message that sometimes you need to welcome the unexpected and trust that there is a reason for a change of plan, to go with the flow and see where it leads.

- Remaining open and aware and creative in the moment.

I suspect the facilitator's top values were respect, trust and empathy. She was definitely living her life aligned to them.

Below is a list of core values commonly used by leadership institutes and programs. This list is not exhaustive, but it will give you an idea of some common core values (also called personal values):

Core Values list

- Authenticity
- Achievement
- Adventure
- Authority
- Autonomy
- Balance
- Beauty
- Boldness
- Compassion
- Challenge
- Citizenship
- Community
- Competency
- Contribution
- Creativity
- Curiosity
- Determination
- Empathy
- Faith

- Friendships
- Fun
- Growth
- Happiness
- Honesty
- Humor
- Influence
- Inner Harmony
- Justice
- Kindness
- Knowledge
- Leadership
- Learning
- Love
- Loyalty
- Meaningful Work
- Openness
- Optimism
- Peace

- Pleasure
- Poise
- Popularity
- Recognition
- Religion
- Reputation
- Respect
- Responsibility
- Security
- Self-Respect
- Service
- Spirituality
- Stability
- Success
- Status
- Trust
- Wealth
- Wisdom

DISCOVER YOUR DNA

It is all well and good to know your values and to understand your leadership type, but the next challenge is knowing how you respond under pressure. What kind of person do you become under pressure and are you okay with that?

It is easy to be a leader when everything is going well. However, when the chips are down and everyone is looking to you for an answer, leadership can really be a lonely, winding track in the wilderness.

What sustains you at this time is: knowing yourself; embracing your values; knowing your attributes; and being happy with who you are. There is no judgement and there is no single, preferable leadership style. We are born with this natural ability. But we need to keep checking in with ourselves to make sure we are still on track.

"We were all born with extraordinary powers of imagination, intelligence, feeling, intuition spirituality and of physical and sensory awareness."

SIR KENNETH ROBINSON

UNLOCK THE CAGE

The unfortunate thing is that most human beings wake up in fear every morning, they look in their bathroom mirror and judge their reflection. Crikey, how old do I look today? Oh no, I'm sure I have lost more hair overnight! Really, who do I think I am, trying to make a difference in the world? Am I good enough? Does my bum look that big?

It is relentless this self-judgement and how does it serve us? To demoralise and depress our spirits, day-in-and day-out. This continual external judgement continues throughout the day, from the newspapers and magazines we read, to the online chatter we might be part of. I marvel at how animals are not affected by any of this. It is exactly as though the more man's evolutionary path has developed, the more pain we cause ourselves. This instant human judgement really saps our energy.

Animals in the wild wake in the morning to face far more daunting challenges than we do. They have to find food and water and stay alive. They are concerned with survival, yet the birds sing sweetly; even when there is thick snow on the ground, they don't seem worried. They seem to have an innate trust that all will be okay. Normally, they will have made contingency plans, storing food and building a form of shelter. However, I don't believe they worry about their relationships or their external image unless courting.

What can we learn from this? How can we free ourselves from this cage of worry and judgement?

"The universe is holding its breath for you to take your place...the unique place in all creation that only you can fill."

DAVID WHYTE

We are the only animals who pay to live on their own planet. The native American Indians never understood that man can claim the earth and can buy land. To them it is free for all living things.

We often spend a lifetime trying to preserve our patch of land, and owning a home is often the main goal. Have we missed something in our human evolution?

Which unique place in the universe do you fill?
How can you set yourself free to achieve this?

CHAPTER 3

ENERGY IS EVERYTHING

HUMANS SEEM TO THINK WE CAN BUY ENERGY across the counter, from, for example, energy bars, energy drinks and energy foods etc., now a trillion-pound industry. But energy is much more complex than our own physicality. We can motivate, disassociate, manipulate and emulate without using a word and without a health drink in sight!

NATURE'S GIFT

A few years ago, I had the rare opportunity to attend a conference given by Julio Olalla of *The Newfield Network*. He is normally based in the United States and when he came to the United Kingdom it was a near perfect opportunity to hear him speak. I say 'near perfect' because I was the proud mother of a three-month-old baby son at the time and I had to make a few decisions. Could I risk taking him along? Would he stay quiet and not disturb other people? I decided it was a risk worth taking.

The first couple of hours flashed by without incident.

However, by mid-morning Julio had picked up on the inconsistent movement around me. He immediately came across to me! At first, I thought he might ask me to leave. Instead, he beamed with delight and welcomed his youngest participant by holding him up for everyone to see! There was a loud, "Aaaaah" from the audience, followed by a gentle clapping. It was as if the whole room had breathed out at the same time.

Why should this tiny scrap of humankind provoke such a loving reaction from a group of total strangers? Could it be that this little baby reminded us of something we have lost; our unconditioned self? His energy – energy of innocence, potential, freedom – touched everyone in the room. He inspired their energy and for a few seconds people remembered their own unlimited potential.

It is a natural gift shared by small children and animals. Without language, they communicate powerful energetic signals through their bodies all the time and they are highly effective at getting their needs met. Research shows that approximately ninety percent of our communication is non-verbal. What is it about this ninety percent that we try to suppress at our own peril? Why do we not embrace this tool for effective communication? It is a physical attribute we need to share with other living things, feeling their energy, picking up their energetic signals through our eyes and hands more than our voices. A baby is vulnerable and yet so powerful!

Animals are the experts in energetic transfer because their life depends on it. They use energy in a myriad of different ways from warning other animals, to transferring vital information from one creature to another. Most animal species have their own vocal languages, ranging in complexity from the simple to the highly sophisticated sonar, which dolphins and whales use. However, they cannot talk and are much more dependent on picking up bodily indicators. They are sentient beings and can use and manipulate other animals simply by using body posture and energy.

I used to live in a city, where my house had a walled garden with a large wooden gate at one end and an old broken iron gate at the other. It contained a small decorative pond not more than six foot in diameter. Imagine my delight when one morning I looked out of the window and there was the unforgettable sight of a fine statuesque wild duck and eleven tiny newly hatched ducklings all floating on my pond. The mother duck had built her nest in a neighbour's garden and then paraded her brood through the broken iron gate to my pond. This squadron of ducks performed this manoeuvre every day. It was a magnificent sight to wake up to every morning.

One particular morning, I was working, deep in thought in my office. My concentration was broken by a huge rumpus in the garden. Fearing the worst, I assumed a cat or fox had found the brood and they were under attack. The mother duck was up on the garden wall flapping and quacking with all her might. I rushed down the stairs and into the garden to find no scoundrel lurking, but that the mother duck had hidden her ducklings under a bush. However, when I counted them there were only ten ducklings, one was missing. The minute the mother duck saw me, she stopped quacking and flew away. I suddenly realized that I had been chosen to become the guardian of ten baby ducklings.

The plot thickened. Where had she gone? Would she come back? What do ducklings eat? An anxious two hours passed. However soon, and to my relief, I once again heard the loud quacking of a wild duck. But this time it came from behind the large wooden gate. I thought to myself – why doesn't she fly over the wall as she did before? However, as I opened the wooden gate the answer stood in front of me. The mother duck had not returned alone, beside her was a precious ball of feathers.

The eleventh duckling had been rescued from some gruesome fate but of course, was unable to scale the garden wall. I became a concierge and opened the gate.

No words were ever spoken. But the duck effectively

conveyed her needs to me and got what she wanted through energetic transfer.

When did humans become experts in disconnection? Why do we tend to push through or override our body's warning signals and push through pain, threat and danger? We seem to be no longer tuned in to our body's intelligence. We live in a world where 'doing' is king and where there is no room for 'being' – staying still for any length of time to contemplate the marvels of our biological makeup.

"Despite the fact that the body is the greatest problem solver there is, quietly and perpetually sustaining life, overcoming billions of obstacles, without our conscious imperatives for it to do so; we don't trust it. Instead, we turn to our medicine cabinets."

DR HERBERT T BENSON

ENERGY INDICATOR

Animals are experts at expanding or conserving energy. Healthy animals rest more than they hunt; learn by play; eat when hungry; don't eat when not hungry; are self-regulating. Some animals store food for the future, but most take each day at a time and live an uncomplicated life.

More than anything, they know how to moderate their output and how to leave something in the tank. For example, a cheetah who has an unsuccessful hunt does not leave herself open to attack by depleting all her reserves; she makes sure there is enough fuel to get herself to a safe place to begin recovery. She has mastered the art of multi-level recovery; sprint-break, sprint-break. She does not try to perform three hunts a day to increase her output or annual yield.

All living beings need the luxury of recovery. How many of us go on holiday and are still plugged in to our devices while in our deckchair by the pool? How does it serve us to be always plugged into the grid?

Energy is everything ... What kind of energy are you bringing to the world?

Whatever energy you bring, people will notice!

REAL PEOPLE LEARNING

A new client has a senior executive team that had plateaued out. Some of the team had been in the same job for twenty years. Valuable knowledge and experience were on a collision course with new markets, new initiatives and incentives, and a sales environment that was demanding change.

The brief was to provide a disruptive experience that would free up new energy; motivate the team to step up and take more responsibility; be more proactive; and open up to new perspectives.

Working with live horses immediately creates a different energetic response from clients; stripped of the power of speech they have to find a different form of communication because horses do not care what job title you hold, what car you drive, or how much money you have in the bank. They are looking for congruent behaviour.

This senior team was outside its comfort zone, with high IQs and impressive CVs. But it was not equipped to deal with this new experience without dialogue.

The horses were not too happy either. Horses will not cooperate if there is any fakery or posturing involved. They have to make razor sharp decisions based on the environment and the energy being transmitted because their lives literally depend on getting it right. The only priorities horses have are: Can I trust you? Am I safe? Who is leading right now?

Energy is the currency. Get it wrong and a horse as a prey animal will flee or refuse to collaborate.

On this particular day, with this specific team, progress was slow. However, significant insights flowed.

For example, understanding energy in business is undervalued; when should I step up – step down – collaborate – take charge – follow, are all vital to a successful business outcome.

As they progressed through the carefully constructed challenges, the team started to show up, energy changed, risks were taken and rules were broken if they were no longer serving the team. The individual spirit and innate leadership qualities started to come to the surface.

Understanding how to change energy and the positive and shadow side to energy gives your team a clear advantage. Once understood, energies can be applied immediately and can turn a team from low motivation to being energised very quickly and effectively.

The transformation of this team was remarkable; without the horses it would have been impossible to truly break down the layers of distrust, the lack of respect and the destructive atmosphere in the workplace in such a short period of time.

The CEO later wrote: "There is something unique about the way the horses reflect back – without ego – exactly what energy you bring and exactly how you are gelling. That day cemented us as a team, more than any other leadership or team building course you can ever have. It is second to none. I highly recommend it."

INSTINCTIVE INSIGHTS

The following instinctive insights were provided as feedback from this team, after their experience with the horses in the paddock.

- What kind of energy can I bring into the workplace?

- Is it appropriate right now?

- How important is it to change the energy to successfully negotiate change?

- What happens when responsibility is rotated?

- Learn from how animals communicate and share for the good of the whole.

- How, when the pressure increases in the wild, the group, team or herd, display a heightened awareness, trust each other, move closer together into a tighter unit, so they can overcome any eventuality?

• What attitude or energy is not serving us right now?

"There are three types of people in this world: adders; subtractors; and multipliers."

SIMON COHEN

Simon informs us that when you are with people who are adders you feel empowered and energized; and your soul smiles a bit more with every encounter.

The subtractors leave you somehow feeling less, subtracted from. As though they take something from you to feed their own energy.

And then there are multipliers. Now, if you are lucky, you might be married to one – or they might be someone you meet only once in your life – and they set off something disproportionate within you; the Multiplier Effect.

It is becoming vital that we understand how to be a multiplier – the world needs people who have come alive with contagious energy, who can dream, inspire and create. People who know that:

Energy + Execution = Extraordinary Results.

What you notice in any company are the levels of energy associated with different projects. In some instances, an initiative may be characterized in terms of energy 'around' it. In others, a team in which ideas flow freely and colleagues work collaboratively and effortlessly, the work will be described as 'high energy'. In other people, a particular influential person may be known as the 'energiser' – someone who can spark progress and drive action with apparent ease.

On the flipside, there seem to always be the people who have an uncanny ability to drain the life out of a group. These energy 'sappers' or energy 'vampires' are to be avoided. They not only drain the people they meet, but often influence and affect the productivity of people they might not even know.

In the business world, we often talk of 'the shadow of the leader.' It is normally seen as a positive shadow where the leader illuminates the lives of their followers. However, a leader can also have a bad or toxic shadow, which can envelop their employees and cause unnecessary stress, leading to a huge energy drain effecting human and company resources.

These leaders:

• abuse power;

- hoard privileges;

- mismanage information;

- act inconsistently;

- misplace or betray loyalties; and

- fail to assume responsibilities.

Consider this famous Native American story.

A white-haired Cherokee is teaching his grandchildren about life. He tells them. "A fight is going on inside of me. A terrible fight and it is a fight between two wolves. One wolf represents fear, greed, hatred, anger, envy, false pride, self-pity, resentment, guilt, inferiority, arrogance, deceitfulness, superiority and selfishness.

The other wolf stands for peace, love, kindness, joy, truth, compassion, humility, transparency, authenticity, friendship, respect, integrity, benevolence, generosity, faith, sharing, serenity and empathy.

The same fight is going on inside you and every other person too."

The children thought about this for a while. Then, one little girl asked her grandfather, "Which wolf will win?"

The old Cherokee held a long silence.

Then, simply said, "Whichever one you feed."

Which wolf inside you will you feed to impact the energetic state of how you come across to everyone you meet?

WHAT IS ENERGY?

Biologically we are great big balls of vibrating energy and it is important to understand how to increase, preserve, nurture and protect this valuable asset. For example, we refer to energy in conversation all the time:

"I'm feeling drained of energy."

"If only I had his boundless energy."

"I connected to the energy in the room."

"I don't know where you get your energy from?"

Energy can show up in a myriad different ways.

NEGATIVE ENERGY SYMPTOMS

1) Compassion fatigue; people so passionate about other people that they often don't look after themselves and place themselves at the bottom of the 'to do list'.

2) Physical depletion, body in chaos; people who are overriding the warning signals and bucking the natural rhythms at their peril.

3) Mental burn out; people who live their lives believing that 'doing' is good with no room for 'being'.

4) Material affluence versus time affluence.

5) Relationship malfunctions.

POSITIVE ENERGY SYMPTOMS

1) Energy attracts energy.

2) Energy creates forward movement.

3) Managing our own energy will impact massively on our lives.

4) Energy allows us to be passionate and creative; and releases us from any constraints.

5) Laughter is a vehicle for transmitting positive energy to other people.

CONTROLLING ENERGY

It is as important to know how to stop as well as how to go. While we acknowledge how powerful the use of high energy can be, we must also recognize there are times when it is vital to slow our energy – to stop, reflect and regenerate our minds and bodies.

We live in an 'always on' society, with the constant noise of information in our work and private lives. What does this do to creativity?

"The brain needs to think and relax, to find head space to come up with solutions and be creative, 'always on' living is blocking that process, stopping thoughts bubbling up to the surface ... we need to give people time alone to get off the grid."

MARTIN RAYMOND

This does not have to involve a lengthy retreat, but can be achieved by changing our approach in small ways to allow contemplation and creativity to return. The creativity which will drive you, your company and your employees onwards and upwards. Research by Amy Cuddy at Harvard Business School* has demonstrated that adopting Power Poses for two minutes can increase levels of testosterone by twenty percent and decrease levels of cortisol by twenty five percent. These results influence how you react to stress or stressful situations and demonstrate that from little tweaks there can be big changes to your life.

Take some quiet time here to reflect about yourself and

*(ref: Power Posing: Brief Nonverbal Displays Affect Neuroendocrine Levels and Risk Tolerance, Association for Psychological Science, 2010)

how you behave at your place of work and with your colleagues, as well as at home with your family and friends.

Replay your life back to five years ago and introduce us to that person you were then.

- How does your energy compare now?

- What were you like?

- What was your passion then?

- What was your personal USP?

- What was your company's USP?

- Were you valued for your contribution?

- Did you have a life?

"Most people are dead at 35; but we don't bury them until they are 75."

BRANDON W JOHNSON

Brandon asks people to, "imagine an organization full of the living dead, just walking around and taking up space … imagine the cost financially and emotionally to every human in that building."

He stated that the "worst thing anyone can do in life is to live it in silence, not doing your part, not giving yourself permission to be you, that if we are not giving our best ... we are holding ourselves back."

"Humans are like waves of potential equipped with a timing device - sometimes the dial gets stuck."

UNKNOWN

You need to be aware of your own personal energy and how you impact the world around you all the time. By understanding how to manage energy you can impact your bottom line. To achieve this state, it requires real, tangible, 'in the moment' insights, and these are best affected by experiential learning situations.

Specific experiential learning will give you real understanding about how your colleagues:

- perform under pressure and how they will respond;
- their leadership style and energy type; and
- their propensity for risk.

It will show you individual and team natural defaults in moments of pressure; how will they move or translate to what is coming next? Also, it will reveal how to manage your energy, to prevent burnout, and how to be instantly empowered and ready for action.

Consider how valuable the answers to these questions would be to you and your team.

AESOP'S FABLES: THE FOX AND THE HEDGEHOG

"The fox knows many things but the hedgehog knows one big thing.

In a vote for the smartest animal on the planet, most people would probably put the fox above the hedgehog. The fox is cunning, quick, sleek and creative. It is tenacious in finding ways to outwit its prey and even in seeking a way to get around the traps and barriers humans put in its way.

The hedgehog on the other hand, though nimble on its feet, seems far less ambitious. A cross between a toothbrush and an anteater, it is mainly concerned with finding food and looking after its nest. Where the fox is sensitive to whatever is happening within the wider environment, the hedgehog seems preoccupied within its own small world, hardly aware of anything beyond the radius of a few meters.

How is it, then, that the hedgehog consistently outsmarts the fox? The fox lies patiently in wait at the crossroads for the unsuspecting hedgehog. And when the hedgehog arrives, the fox makes a move with speed, stealth and guile from a cunning angle of attack. But the hedgehog senses the approach and with a minimum amount of fuss, rolls himself up into a perfectly defended spiky ball, which denies the fox any chance of success.

The fox retreats, baffled, and slinks off into the forest to develop some newer, even more creative stratagems. But, despite his cunning, creativity, speed and slyness, the fox hardly ever wins. Despite his many cunning he can't overcome the hedgehog's one simple, unadorned, yet efficient strategy. This battle, in some form or other, is played out every day. And almost every time the hedgehog wins."

I include this fable because it clearly illustrates you don't have to always use high-voltage energy to achieve results. It is a matter of choosing what strategy and what energy is appropriate right now and knowing naturally what choice to make.

The fox has much knowledge, is fast, creative and cunning, so we assume that the smartest thinking or actions will triumph. However, the hedgehog has self-knowledge; he knows his strengths, his energy levels, his unique traits and his purpose, so he is ultimately the winner ...

How much value do you place on being energetically connected to your purpose right now?

CHAPTER 4

RUNNING WITH THE PACK

AS HUMAN BEINGS WE SAY; "If you want to travel fast, go alone, if you want to travel far, go together." However, animals know something else; if you want to travel safely be part of a herd or a pack.

It is a fundamental requirement for most prey animals in the wild to travel in herds or packs. If we take a prey animal, for example horses, they move in huge herds. To be isolated out on the prairie means certain death. A lone horse will be picked off quickly by coyotes, wolves or similar. They have each other's backs. They support each other when under duress. They give each other a chance to rest by being vigilant, while the others in the herd sleep. They scratch and groom each other, reaching those places that are out of reach for the individual and which might cause irritation or become infected. They communicate in different ways, from sonar in whales and dolphins, to the deep rumble and vibrations that is the language of elephants. They scan the body to understand meaning and intention and they are masters of energetic transfer. Animals have ways of transmitting information to each other that man is yet to translate, but it is clear that in their behaviour they comfort each other (I'm here). They protect (Back off now). They sound the alert (Danger approaching) and they call to their young (Stay close).

This is such an important trait for humans to understand whether it be in one's personal, work environment or playing a sport or belonging to any team. The feeling of someone 'having your back' and having someone else's back is almost old fashioned in concept, but builds exceptional loyalty. Ask anyone who has been in the Armed Forces and they will tell you how exquisite it feels.

I am not simply talking about physical safety, but psychological safety as well.

Do you remember that feeling in your life when someone had your back? That feeling of sweet release, that precious support at a very crucial time.

PINSTRIPED SUITS

I sold my first company to a dynamic PLC. It was an exciting time in my life, a huge step up in many ways. But I embraced the challenge of implementing my company into a large PLC with energy and positivity.

The first few months passed in a blur of activity, the steep learning curve of integrating our systems into a much larger organisation and the scale of the database provided many interesting challenges. For example, we moved from 4,000 to 140,000 customers. However, it was the culture of a PLC that was a mystery to me and caused me the most angst.

How was it possible for a company with so many employees in the sport and leisure industry to be so rife with dissatisfaction, lack of trust, lack of support and suspicion of each other? After all, we were trying to create a product that gave our customers a dream lifestyle, fun and was leading edge. Surely, we were all working for the good of the whole – not so it would seem!

As my confusion mounted, I began to feel that my team was becoming more and more isolated from the main organisation. I decided to do something about this. Looking back, it now seems hilarious. However, at the time I was shocked by the results.

Our new brochure was due to be sent out to the 140,000 customers and I decided to give the other departments in the organisation a chance to preview our brochure and provide feedback. We decided to meet and greet all staff entering the building first thing in the morning with a free hot coffee and a Danish pastry, plus a copy of our new brochure. My team were there in the foyer as people started to arrive. Well, the reactions were extreme. We could almost detect which department people worked in by the reaction to our gesture and some people were downright hostile.

"If I had wanted a coffee, I would have bought it myself."

"I have no time for this, have you any idea how busy my morning is?"

Some people simply walked straight past us without a word.

Other people were delighted.

"What a nice idea, I look forward to looking at your brochure later."

"Great, I wondered what you guys were up to."

It was at the same time that I began to feel hostility in the boardroom. It was overt – along the lines of 'did you see the football last night conversations' that I could not contribute to – or speaking in a jargon that left me intimidated. I was not a trained accountant and therefore some language I did not understand. I was definitely not part of their tribe. My ideas were crushed before they could germinate and I felt my confidence and passion draining away as each board meeting passed. I was not one of them. I talked differently, I dressed differently and my gender and agenda were different.

The question was: How could I combat this slow erosion of my character, and my passion? Well, by wearing a pinstriped suit of course! I thought if I looked like them maybe it would help! Overnight I changed my wardrobe to sterile grey suits.

I hope you are laughing at this moment, because I am!

Can you identify with this story?

Have you ever tried to tone down your identity to fit in?

Have you ever felt the essence of you is being eroded?

Luckily for me, the CEO had his hand on my back. He recognised the value of my brochure experiment in the foyer. How it had shown up the real cultural energy blocks in his company and the lack of clarity especially around direction and communication. Of course, he laughed at my grey suit and reiterated the value of new innovative ideas. The logic behind this was straightforward. The PLC had bought me for a reason – to bring and initiate new products. They needed new blood, not cloned thinking and that was the reason I was of value.

How would it serve anyone if I played the same game?

MIGRATION AWAY FROM OUR NATURAL INSTINCTS

I like to think that the human population recognises the need to be part of a community. However, I fear that the real epidemic in our culture is disconnection from other people, mainly due to the speed at which we live and the increase of technology and time saving gadgets. We are spawning a new generation of isolated and disconnected people. I call it 'the head down generation'. We are becoming more and more separate from the natural world that surrounds us. We are very quickly losing our special survival instincts and awareness that have kept us safe for so long.

Animals too are losing survival instincts. For countless centuries sheep and cattle have been 'hefted' to the poorest and most difficult land in the country. Hefting means to hold livestock without fences, on a mountain or fell. They are taught a sense of belonging by their mothers in their first summer, a system of livestock husbandry based on territorial instinct. They know the routes to the best pastures and where danger lies in the form of wetlands and bogs. Man has now interfered with this innate knowledge by wintering livestock in barns and outbuildings so this knowledge is no longer retained. When the sheep, cattle and horses are returned to the land, they get lost and wander aimlessly. Is there a danger of OUR instinct becoming extinct, and will we as a race be left wandering just as aimlessly?

COLLABORATION

What experiences in nature can we draw on to demonstrate the importance of community, co-operation and shared skill? We all know about the amazing collaborative skills of many types of animals, including lions, dolphins, elephants, wolves and chimpanzees, mainly thanks to the legendary television programs and films of David Attenborough.

Take wolves, they are probably the closest species to man due to their beauty, adaptability and toughness. Also, the wolf pack is highly-social and expressive with distinctive characters. The way they divide labour during a kill to gain the competitive advantage, their loyalty, and their brutality all mirror Man's characteristics. The male wolf also helps raise the young to full maturity and protects the females from attack. Wolves are without doubt a highly functioning and co-operative unit.

THE WAGGLE DANCE

However, my favourite flying insects for demonstrating the power of communication and teamwork in the animal kingdom must be the bees with their famous waggle dance.

Have you ever wondered how bees communicate where the food source is? Well, the answer is that the worker bees inform thousands of their co-workers where the source of the nectar is by performing a dance. Sometimes these locations can be hundreds of feet from the hives, but the colony is on the lookout for nectar and pollen and they need an efficient way of communicating this information with their fellow bees. When navigating, the bee uses the sun as a fixed reference point. This allows them to fly in a compass direction simply by keeping the angle between the lines of light and the sun constant. The bee who is successful in finding a source of nectar will share the location by dancing.

The waggle dance is based on a figure of eight movement. First, the bee moves is an angle indicating the direction of the flowers in relation to the sun. Secondly, the bee waggles its abdomen rapidly and the more it waggles the further the distance. Thirdly, the pollen the bee has collected provides a scent cue for the other bees to smell for and follow.

The bees have found a way to communicate clearly and effectively to the benefit of the whole team. What can we learn from the animal kingdom to help our own communication skills?

REAL PEOPLE, REAL LEARNING

About a year ago, I was working with a CEO whose company was very successful. The context for the session was communication – a very challenging problem in most organisations and in life generally. I particularly wanted this client to 'feel' leadership rather than think strategically.

Our meeting took place at my farm where we are lucky enough to have space to play with ideas outside in nature. I obtained his permission to work without the sense of sight or language; in other words to blindfold my client and work without speech. I proceeded to lead him outside using different techniques. Firstly, I was collaborative and supportive giving him my arm and guiding him with care. Secondly, I gave him the end of a rope to hold and quickened my pace and distance, taking him out of his comfort zone. Thirdly, I went behind him and pushed him gently into the unknown. This carried on until I had exhausted all the different leadership styles that I knew. What he didn't know was that he was moving towards a horse. Finally, I took him into the outdoor arena and placed his hands on the withers of one of my horses.

What happened next will stay with me, and him, forever.

The expression on his face was unbelievable as he felt the strong warm coat of a living thing. He buried his head in the horse's side and he wept. His sense of relief was palpable. The strength and sheer presence of that unmoving horse standing strong and patient by his side was immensely poignant. Another living creature 'had his back' and somehow the horse understood that the man simply needed to be in contact with him and needed support. My thoroughbred horse did not move a muscle. The client was able to let go of his own power for a minute and simply be. To take a breath, feel the moment and gain the insight that it gave him, without words, without sight; simply feeling the animal connection and shared understanding.

During our debrief, I asked him whether he was happy to share this powerful moment. There was no embarrassment or hesitation.

"I was born in the high mountains of Pakistan, where nature in all its glory is on your doorstep. Connection with all living things had been part of the culture. How far away all that seems now, I had forgotten that deep connection and how much I long for that in my life again."

He voiced the central issue that had bought him to work with me in the first place.

"I knew something was unfulfilled in my life. I now know that the way I am living has to change dramatically. I had all the trappings of success, but no idea why I felt this emptiness inside."

Later, he told me: "The most liberating aspect of this course was that I changed my life. I re-valued the way I conducted my business and I bought in a senior manager who now runs the day to day operations and has freed me up to connect with nature and I have found this to be a wonderful bedrock of ideas. I am now positioned to utilise my natural creativity and have someone else handle the daily process for me. Our company has gone from strength to strength."

INSTINCTIVE INSIGHTS

- This was what I call 'breakdown to breakthrough learning'; natural learning using both the man and the animal's Natural Intelligence. This memorable anchor will stay with my client forever.

- Communication is so much more than simply verbal. Leadership comes in many different styles. How do you lead and how does it make people feel?

- We all need support; we are not meant to be independent and isolated. How does it feel when you know that someone has your back and how can you give this to other people?

Access to nature is intrinsic to a high quality of life.

BROKEN DREAM

My own personal story of 'breakdown to breakthrough' allowed me to hold the space for the client mentioned above.

I recognised his deep pain and had experienced similar issues. That significant moment when your deep knowing surfaces and you have a choice to take stock or revert back to your current existence. I am now unsurprised that these momentous moments often take place when we are in natural surroundings. I love the work of Mac Macartney, international speaker, writer and change maker and this particular talk resonated with me:

"When the wise men of the past were gaining deep wisdom, to share with the world," Mac says, "we don't mention that Gautama Buddha received his wisdom whilst sitting underneath a Bodhi Tree; that Muhammad had his revelation in a cave; that Moses went up a mountain to receive the ten commandments from God; and Jesus went to a Judaean desert for forty nights."

Why do we never question the part of nature in these stories?

This does not mean you become a stable hand or a full-time gardener, but make adjustments that will create balance. Balance is essential in life.

My moment with nature happened on Exmoor, up on the top of the moor with the sun setting and the wild ponies grouping together at the beginning of a cold night. I broke down. I had no idea where the emotion had come from or why, but that breakdown moment for me signified the end of my marriage, the end of my corporate life and an end to my life in a capital city. I recognised that something else needed to emerge that had been dormant for a long time and I had no idea where this would lead me, but I knew it would be okay.

HIGHER BEING

This is a new world, where we are separating ourselves from the herd and nature, a world that values independence, freedom and self-sufficiency. A world, which suggests that separating ourselves will develop our propensity to be a higher being. But in doing so do we think it is serving mankind?

"Beware of dysfunctional independence! Every self-made man, brave entrepreneur, original thinker, and solo adventurer has depended on support for their success."

DR ROBERT HOLDEN

We are social hierarchical creatures. We fear rejection or exclusion. We are distinct individuals who generally like to contribute to the success of the whole. So, why are we trying to go it alone? Surely this path of competition rather than collaboration will bring more stress, more unhappiness and more mental health problems. This self-imposed separation is making us more vulnerable rather than stronger.

I hear people talking about getting out into nature to recalibrate and re-balance. But we are nature – how can we be separate from self?

Running with the pack is not about being a clone, or losing your individuality. It is about celebrating your strengths and bringing all of you to the table. Nature is a celebration of diversity, where prey and predator exist side by side. When wolves are satiated, they play. All are included, the young, old, scarred, alpha – the entire pack successfully relaxes. They become the strength of their diversity and they know that.

FIND YOUR PRIDE

Where do you belong?

For our young people the pressure is high to conform. Branded clothing is an expectation, visual labels that declare

'I belong to the right tribe', along with digitally enhanced photos of themselves online. Comfort zone comes from being normal. They are frightened of being different. Peer group success is often judged on the possession of things. The newspapers, social media, magazines focus on material things. We are being led down the road of human beings being fundamentally selfish. It is all about 'me' and what 'I' can get. This stockpiling of things will get me noticed and make me popular. However, the opposite is actually true – this will only breed dissatisfaction and isolation.

Dr Robert Holden's girl's prayer demonstrates this point beautifully:

"Our cash
Which art on plastic
Hallowed be thy name
Thy Cartier watch
Thy Prada bag
In Harrods as it is in Selfridges
Give us each day our Platinum Visa
And forgive us our overdraft
As we forgive those who stop our Master card
And lead us not into Next
And deliver us from Benetton

But neither is the Cartier, the Dior and the Armani
For Chanel No 5 and eternity
Amex."

I believe this message needs to be overturned. The degree of social interaction that humans demonstrate is second to no other species; altruism and empathy in humankind exceeds all other creatures. Love, laughter, learning and giving are innate and embedded in our DNA. Business is not always 'dog eat dog', competitive and ruthless. There are examples all around us of inspirational people and businesses flourishing in a co-creative environment. The message must not be 'self-maximising man' but 'pride in the creativity and difference one brings to the group'.

Diversity is the lifeblood of innovation. When you find your tribe, or your pride, you will be unstoppable. All of you will be appreciated, and that inclusive environment will give you and your business an enviable sense of identity.

"What connects a tribe or a pack is a common commitment to the thing they feel born to do. This can be extraordinarily liberating, especially if you've been pursuing your passion alone."

SIR KENNETH ROBINSON

Remember the bees? How often are you dancing the Waggle Dance?

CHAPTER 5

ROCKY ROAD

POLO IS A SPORT THAT GRABS YOU by the throat and doesn't let go! Addictive, dangerous, racy, with huge sex appeal. It is a sport where you haemorrhage money, on a par with motor racing. It is renowned for fast living and a spicy social life. At the top of the game, there are professional players from all walks of life.

However, most of the players at the top level are Argentinian. The person sponsoring the team is called a Patron and the Patron will pay for the whole entourage, including: grooms; horses; equipment; and the players. For the professional players, if you are injured or not picked to play, you don't get paid; their life is definitely a rocky road.

SO, WHAT HAPPENED TO JACK?

For Jack, entrance to the England Team gave him some stability, but no entrance pass to the preserve of the very rich. He had to provide all the transport for his horses, vet's fees, stabling, and training out of his own pocket;

and he was always the poor relation. The world of glitz and glamour was lost on Jack. His desire was to play polo to the best of his ability. The trappings of wealth did not appeal. However, he was on course to make his dream a reality.

But on one fateful day, all his dreams came crashing down around him. Late for a match, he pulled onto the hard shoulder of a dual carriageway because his horsebox was broken down. With not long to go before the start of an important match, he had no alternative but to climb under the horsebox to repair a part that was falling off.

While working under the heavy vehicle, something went horribly wrong with the hydraulics on the ramp at the back and one and a half tons of metal landed on his spine. He broke his pelvis in three places. He was lucky to come out alive. However, he spent the next eighteen months flat on his back in bed while he slowly healed.

These moments define us. These moments of gut-wrenching agony, piercing us to the core, when all the wheels come off and you feel like you are in freefall, utterly disbelieving of what has happened. There is no hiding from this moment. We will all face the rocky road in our lifetime. The lonely walk that only you can make. That dark night of the soul. How do you stay on the road and not fall off the cliff into the abyss?

The answer is with courage and adaptability. Those two concepts are the mantra for the survival of all living creatures on this planet.

Our DNA has evolved to give us great reservoirs of courage and adaptability to navigate life in our hour of need. Struggle, hardship, heartache are the situations we try to protect ourselves, our children and our loved ones from and that is natural. But perhaps instead of trying to shield ourselves and other people from struggle and inevitable pain, we should be fanning the flames of courage and adaptability; digging deep wells into those reservoirs to give sustenance for the journey ahead.

Jack went on to make a full recovery, the determination to fulfill his dream giving him the courage and strength to fight back to full fitness.

COTTON WOOL

Once I bought a Butterfly Garden for my five-year-old son. It came in a kit form, with live bugs that we introduced into the garden so we could watch them grow. All went well and each chrysalis developed normally and began to hatch. All except one, which seemed to mature more slowly than the others. I kept my eye on it – it really seemed to be struggling – and at one point its movement stopped altogether.

That afternoon when my son returned from school, I thought maybe if I helped it to get free of the paper sack where it was still attached it would speed up the process. Maybe it would catch up to the other butterflies. As soon as I removed the sack, I understood my error. The butterfly was misshapen. The wings were too small for its body and it quickly died. Why? Because an emerging butterfly needs to struggle to force fluid from its body to its wings. It is critical for its development and there is no shortcut. Exactly like our lives, challenge and struggle are natural and inevitable to learn and grow stronger. We need to have challenges to teach us important life skills. We need this preparation for all that life throws at us. If we try to shortcut this process, we will not learn how to overcome and be resilient.

Sometimes, we try to protect those people around us from these challenges and these struggles, especially those we love. In taking challenges away we do not protect our loved ones or our colleagues; instead we take away their opportunities to grow.

"Opposition is a natural part of life. Just as we develop our physical muscles through overcoming opposition – such as lifting weights – we develop our character muscles by overcoming challenges and adversity."

STEPHEN R COVEY

In the wild, it is not always the strong who survive, but the adaptable. There are so many examples from business where strong brands have disappeared through lack of adaptability and their inability to ride the rocky road. David Attenborough's powerful programs loved by everyone, show the tremendous courage of animals defending their territory, their food, their young and their mates, from what seems like a certain death. We only need to look at nature to be inspired by these qualities. And to understand the hugely motivational stories of animals adapting to new circumstances and surviving despite severe famine, environmental disaster, drought, bushfire, tsunami, loss of habitat and man's destruction.

For example, leopards are not only among the most beautiful animals in Africa, but they are champions of adaption when fitting in, with a change in habitat or environment.

One I read about was found in an abandoned football stadium living with two cubs, eating garbage and chasing pets through the neighbourhood.

Hummingbirds build nests in the same tree where hawks are nesting confident that they can evade capture by their flying prowess. They know lesser predators will not risk coming close to nesting hawks. A dangerous, but courageous strategy.

How does a lobster grow bigger, when its shell is so hard? The only way is for the lobster to shed its shell at regular intervals when its body begins to feel cramped inside the shell. The lobster naturally looks for a reasonably safe spot to rest, while the hard shell comes off and the pink membrane inside forms the basis of the new shell. No matter where a lobster goes for the shedding process, it is vulnerable. It can get tossed against the coral reef or eaten by a fish. The lobster has to risk its life to grow.

We can all identify with the story from our childhood by Hans Christian Anderson, *The Ugly Duckling* who despite torment and ridicule, transformed into the beautiful swan.

The wilderness and the corporate world have many similarities. How beneficial would it be for the corporate world to learn from nature? In some areas, such as product engineering and medicine it is already happening, but in the area of personal leadership and team leadership, this opportunity has not been developed until now!

These motivational stories and inspirational films that we watch about nature's torturous and tumultuous times, give us hope, strength and a memorable anchor to cling to, when the shit hits the fan.

CONSTRUCTIVE CONSCIOUSNESS

Imagine yourself without arms. You cannot hug your children, wrap your fingers around a warm cup of tea and experience the joys of touch. Imagine yourself without legs. You cannot run for the train, you cannot dance or take a walk on the beach with your loved one. How would your life change? How would your very experience of the world around you be different?

Nick Vujicic, Serbian-Australian Christian evangelist and motivational speaker, was born with the rare *Tetra-Amelia Syndrome*, and lives exactly that life. Born without arms and legs, Nick's life could have been one of withdrawal, despair and disappointment. Turned away from mainstream schools, bullied by his peers, Nick could easily have given up. As a child, he fought loneliness, despair and depression. As young as eight, Nick contemplated suicide. He tried to drown himself in eight inches of water. However, his love for his parents was too strong; it stopped him and saved his life. So many times, Nick could have made the choice to give in, to choose a life hiding from the world – or worse.

Instead, Nick found the courage to embrace his life as it was handed to him. He went to university and earned a Bachelor Degree. He now travels the globe experiencing everything the world has to offer; experiencing it his way.

By embracing the world around him, not with his arms, but with his heart, he has found acceptance, welcome and companionship in every corner of the world.

But there is more to Nick. Instead of letting his disability become a disadvantage, he has turned it into something very special; not only for him, but for everyone he meets. He travels the world sharing his inspirational story, bringing hope and encouragement to those people who need it most. Instead of withdrawing to a life hiding indoors, away from the world, he appears in front of crowds of thousands of people, embracing his disability and sharing his courage, his strength and his inspiration.

It is very easy – especially when we have a bad day or face hardship or disappointment – to withdraw from the world around us. But when we do that, we do ourselves a great disservice. We risk missing out on all we can be because of one setback. We have inside each of us the courage to shake off our disappointments and to move on; to put them behind us and focus on the next achievement.

The idea of constructive consciousness came from a wonderful book by Tobias Harwood called, *Great Traits*. He identified three specific examples of how people who have suffered horrific injuries and trauma overcame their personal difficulties through constructive thinking.

- **Mindfulness;** living in the moment, being present and appreciative.

- **Turning adversity into opportunity;** being able to reframe a situation.

- **Interpretation of luck;** opportunities are presented throughout your life and out of these you create your own luck.

Right now, the world needs people to step up and lead with courage and adaptability. Young people need to be brave, resourceful and inventive. Our education system needs to foster innovation, such as outside the box thinking, creativity, and diversity of thinking.

> **The life blood of any business is courage and adaptability to the market trends.**

If you are not moving forward, you are dying, stagnating; and you sign your own death warrant, as many companies have done in the past.

"Remember that sometimes not getting what you want is a wonderful stroke of luck."

THE 14TH DALAI LAMA

THE FEAR CULTURE

Courage in this climate of the unknown, can be the vital ingredient or virtue that a leader or team needs. It is the life force of a business.

"Followers want leaders who make decisions decisively, but inclusively, interpret situations with rational and emotional intelligence and exude confidence and humility."

BILL TREASURER

In business we also need people who have the courage to take the initiative, who have faith in people's abilities, who will raise difficult issues, who will share unpopular opinions and pursue pioneering efforts. They will definitely impact your company's bottom line and boost the morale of your workforce. These people will challenge the status quo and when necessary, break the rules.

Aristotle called courage the first virtue because it made all of the other virtues possible. In business, courage is the backbone that influences all areas of the business, whether it be:

- **Innovation** – pursuing new ideas where often failure comes before success;
- **Sales** – coping with rejection and staying resilient;

- **Customer service** – dealing with the angry or irate customer; or

- **Negotiating** a massive takeover deal.

All of these virtues require us to dig deep. Everyone has the capacity to be courageous. The blocker, of course, can be fear. The fear of being impolite or being seen as a disrupter in the office or in society. Fear is generally seen as a negative attribute, but sometimes it is exactly what we need.

REAL PEOPLE, REAL LEARNING

Working with a family business, or a husband and wife partnership is not for the faint-hearted! Family businesses and partnerships are notoriously sensitive and volatile. Energy blocks are often hidden within the layers of historic baggage. Negotiating this tangle can be extremely rewarding, but the politics can also be suffocating.

The experiential style and non-threatening environment that is created with the horses allow clients to operate naturally as they would in the workplace. They can't hide, or fake the outcome.

Working through specific challenges with the horses, grievances can be released very quickly and often very passionately.

The clients for this programme were a husband and wife team running a well-established and successful management consultancy. They had been experiencing significant problems with client procurement. They were always in the last three preferred suppliers; however they were not managing to cross the line and close the deal. Sales were taking a nosedive and so was their relationship. They were most definitely on rocky terrain.

However, they had the courage to accept that something needed to change.

The brief was to identify the road blocks; to re-energise and re-motivate the jaded partnership; and to create a positive action plan, which celebrated their individual strengths and would allow them to increase sales.

It was clear this couple had completely different agendas; their vision, energy and leadership styles were polar opposites. This point of difference had obviously served them well in the past, but now had become an irritant. Watching them interacting with the horses was truly illuminating and almost painful at the same time.

The woman's response to the challenge was to move forward at a colossal pace with huge determination to complete the task. Her focus was on the goal and she positioned herself out in front. There was clearly no interest or consideration for her team who were bringing up the rear.

The man's response couldn't have been more different. He was almost stationary, building a wonderful rapport with his equine team, building trust without any awareness of time, goal setting or forward momentum.

In her frustration to deliver an outcome, the woman almost carried the team around the arena, which was exhausting to watch.

Her husband's reaction was palpable. How dare she bully and ride over everyone to achieve results. This is what she always did in the business. I feel inhibited, humiliated and neglected as a member of the team. There is no care being taken, simply a focus on getting the job done – we need a result.

This one challenge gave them a rich reservoir of information and insights they could take back into the boardroom and work on in the weeks ahead.

Their joint feedback said it all: "This day heightened the sense of how we were relating to each other in our business. It allowed us to value our diversity, reduce conflict and to be more effective. Within six months we added 20% to our bottom line and we have never looked back."

INSTINCTIVE INSIGHTS

- How does courage serve the business long-term?

- Build respect for different skill sets.

- Celebrate strengths.

- Share different perspectives.

- Safety; how safe do I need to feel?

- Redistribution of roles.

- Importance of boundaries with employees and customers.

- Energetic transfer.

- Rotational leadership.

All of these learnings can be combined and included within the Model of Appreciative Enquiry, which helped my clients with the forward planning of their business. This model is available on the N-stinctive website – www.n-stinctive.com

MAKE A STAND

Sometimes on the rocky road we hit a road block, which is so insurmountable it requires us to make a stand. This can be uncomfortable and unpopular with your team and often conflicts with your own personal values. It can sometimes mean that your time with an organisation is finished and you need to have the courage to move on. It is the pothole that makes you swerve and change track.

It always demonstrates courage and leadership and yet can cause you to be extremely unpopular at the time.

Can you remember being thirteen years old?

At that age you just want to fit in. You don't want any fuss. You don't want anything embarrassing to happen. And you certainly don't want anyone to see you with your parents. Imagine how excruciating this would be if all of this occurred at the same time, which is what happened to me at the age of thirteen.

I was with my parents and sister at the theatre watching a production of *Accidental Death of an Anarchist* by Dario Fo. My dad had been in the Royal Air Force during the war and was extremely patriotic and proud to be British.

The play is about the troubled times in Ireland and the different factions, their views, values and beliefs. The first half of the play outlines the perspective of the Irish Republican Army and was blistering in its attack on the British forces.

Suddenly from nowhere my father was on his feet in a very packed theatre. He started to berate the actors on the stage: "I will not sit in a British theatre and listen to you badmouthing the brave men and women who fight for our freedom."

The play was stopped dead in its tracks, but the cast on the stage at that moment were amazing. They thanked my father for his outburst and his passion and invited him to stay for the second half, when the tables would be turned. They were glad that their acting had caused such a powerful reaction.

Meanwhile the thirteen-year old me was cowering under the theatre seat.

But now, looking back at this incident, I am so proud that my father had the courage to challenge something he felt so passionate about. Even if his outburst offended some sensibilities.

What is it you will make a stand for on your rocky road?

CHAPTER 6

LIFE FORCE

STAY IN YOUR POWER

IF I WAS ASKED TO GIVE A USEFUL PIECE of advice to anyone it would be, "stay in your power". This is not the same as being 'on purpose' or 'staying power', which we will look at next. No doubt you're asking, how do I know what my power is? This is not the power of dominance, authority, birth-right, money, title or position. These are external, man-made labels. And it is not what you do for a living or your passion. I am talking about your essence, your inner compass, the internal life force that brings you alive. It is the centre of your personal power, the connection with a deep knowing that you can trust to lead you into creativity and flow; the place where you are happy in your own skin.

We are all born with our essence and personal power already assembled; if you don't believe me ask any parent. But are we born powerless? Absolutely not, a combination of life force plus essence, has the parents scrambling to provide everything the newborn needs.

It is what you bring into the room with you; what you transmit without speaking. If you are struggling to locate your essence, delve deep into that little girl or boy that you once were. What do you see? Once you clearly see your essence, you will naturally fight for what brings you wonder and joy; and what makes your juices flow.

I look at my son and his power is kindness. I look at my daughter and her power is being a safe pair of hands for other people. It is where you excel in human traits; oozing out of every pore. Mother Theresa's essence for example, was her deep compassion. When you know your essence, you come into your power and you can influence and affect change effortlessly.

When you stay in your power, no one can take it away, or touch you with criticism, rhetoric or judgement, because what other people think is irrelevant to you. You know that your essence is your power and it is your anchor that gives you tremendous strength and solace; and a deep-rooted stability and belief in self.

REAL PEOPLE, REAL LEARNING

I happened to be working with a senior women's leader group. One of the group had been knocked off balance in her career because she had accepted a role in her organisation that did not match her essence. The position was flattering – more money, more status – and there had been much peer group pressure for her to accept this new job. However, in reality, she felt exposed, totally outside her comfort zone and under pressure to make strategic decisions that she felt were not correct. The outcome was that in a short space of time, her personal power and leadership style had been severely undermined and she was suffering.

Working outside in nature and with other living creatures – horses – the learning comes thick and fast.

The client challenge set on this particular day, although relatively simple, had a profound impact on this female leader. I asked her to walk with a horse of her choice around a course that involved four pillars.

There was no instruction on how to do this, the delegate had to dig deep and perform the challenge in a way that felt most natural to her. Interestingly, she walked shoulder to shoulder with the horse in a collaborative way. The challenge was completed in a relaxed and congruent manner.

I then asked her to lead the horse at the far extremity of the lead rope, way ahead of the horse, and report back to the group on her findings.

We repeated the exercise walking with the horse still at the front end but this time with support from a couple of her colleagues.

The insights began to flow and the relief she experienced was huge. She now understood why her confidence had plummeted and how to match her job to her innate strengths.

The CEO who recommended she take the course said: "When she first started working with us she was competent, but not confident. The confidence level she has risen to since that day has been unbelievable and she cites this as the anchor experience for her really owning her power and being able to delegate and fully manage her career effectively. It is highly recommended for anyone who wants to bring their staff together and tap into the natural talents of their team – which sometimes as the leader you do not see."

INSTINCTIVE INSIGHTS

- Leadership comes in many different styles.
- What style of leadership is appropriate right now?

- Do my innate leadership skills match what is required?

- Faking it is not tolerated in the wild because it will cause death and uncertainty and affect the stability of the group.

- In business faking it causes stress, exhaustion and fear of exposure.

- Know what it is that you bring to the table.

- Stay in this knowing and don't allow other people to influence you.

- Gain confidence and celebrate what you stand for.

- Understand the power of intention.

- Understand your personal power.

- When you are being you, everyone wins.

AUTHENTICITY

In business the phrase, 'authentic business' or 'authentic leadership' is popular at the moment. This is not something that appears overnight; it takes a lot of work to uncover this buried treasure. The following questions will help you focus on your own authenticity.

- Can you remember the real reason you created this business?

- What is the essence of your creation?

- Can you remember the real reason you took this job?

- Has the job lived up to your expectation? Is the essence of you flourishing in your work environment?

Perhaps your original true desire was to create a financially sustainable business that creates jobs for people and makes a difference in the world. You wanted passionate and motivated people working in your teams who express their creativity without fear. But many of us lose sight of that goal, not through a lack of vision, but in doubting our personal power to achieve it.

What is extraordinary about animals is that they never doubt their personal power, not for a moment. Not simply because they have sharp claws and powerful jaws. Look into their eyes and see what comes back at you – be prepared to be blown away.

The wonderful wildlife photographer Daniel Fox captures the beauty of that look in his work.

"When I photograph wildlife, I don't hide from them. I want them to see me. I don't want to be a visitor. I want to connect and be present. I don't want to humanize and beautify them. I want to honour and recognize their spirit. I want to meet their gaze and share that deep ancestral sense of commonality we have."

How do we give away our personal power in our relationships and in our businesses? Judgement by ourselves or other people can stifle our life force, taking away our confidence and our *joie de vivre* and our natural initiative. Alternatively, seeking approval from other people can become our gaoler. Approval can't be trusted, it can be taken away at any time. It keeps us small and constantly striving. We can mould ourselves into what other people expect us to be but we will lose our core identity in the process.

"Don't succumb to paralysis by over-analysis if it looks like a duck and it quacks like a duck, it's a duck, right? I'm not going to take a duck's feathers and send them away for DNA analysis only to find out 10 weeks later that it was a duck because by then it's bloody well flown away anyway!"

STUART ROSE

Being polite and not wanting to offend also constrains us. Even when we know or can smell danger, we sometimes override this with our political correctness and love of protocol. A wonderful example of this is in the film, *The Girl With The Dragon Tattoo*, when the main protagonist accepts an offer of a drink from a man he knows is a cold blooded killer. He overrides his gut instinct to his detriment. Animals never do this; they don't have the ability to fake their reaction and they don't trade parts of themselves for approval.

We make ourselves less whole by doing this. However, these parts of us that we trade for approval are not lost, they are merely hidden and they can be accessed anytime in the future.

"One of the most dramatic manifestations of the life force is seen in the plant kingdom. When times are harsh and what is needed to bloom cannot be found, certain plants become spores. These plants dampen down and wall off their life force to survive. It is an effective strategy. Spores found in mummies, spores thousands of years old, have unfolded into plants when given the opportunity of nurture. Imagine that, being able to put your life force on hold indefinitely. I expect many people are applying this strategy in their lives. Through constant judgement, criticism and a toxic environment they hide away the true and unique self and stay that way throughout their whole life. A spore is a survival strategy, not a way of life. Spores do not grow. They endure. What you need to do to survive may be very different from what you need to live."

DR RACHEL NAOMI REMEN

The greatest gift you can give yourself is the permission to be you. Imagine how many people and organisations are not reacning their potential because they are stuck in a 'spore' state.

STAYING POWER OR TRUE GRIT

This is a very different concept. This is resilience or staying power in the face of adversity. We have many stories from the wild and the animal kingdom, which demonstrate this point. There are a selection of examples below; see which one resonates with you the best.

There are more than 10,000 different species of ants and ant strengths vary considerably. Most ants can carry more than three times their weight and can survive in the water for twenty-four hours by forming a living raft. When they are placed in water they constantly move around or rotate to ensure that no ant is underneath the water for too long. It is possible for them to be in this form for weeks or a month if necessary, until they find a suitable place for the colony to settle. The thing that defines the ant is it represents ten percent of all animal tissue on the planet.

Camels are built for survival. They can live for six months without a meal and a month without water. One of the reasons they survive such high temperatures is because of the fat in their humps, which means they do not break sweat until their body temperature is more than forty-one degrees. They can hydrate faster than any other species, being capable of drinking thirty gallons of water in only thirteen minutes! If any other animal drank water that quickly, they would dilute their blood and kill themselves.

The 2005 documentary film, *March of the Penguins* highlighted the toughness and resilience of the Emperor Penguin. Every year the adult penguin of breeding age makes a sixty-mile journey to the breeding ground. The penguins only have one partner – the female lays one egg and rolls it to the male penguin to incubate. The females then set out to find food and do not return for two months. During this time, the males huddle together in large groups to retain heat, keeping the eggs warm beneath them. They stay together and they rotate; this technique is necessary for their survival because they endure temperatures as low as minus seventy degrees. By the time the females return the males have not eaten for four months and have lost half their bodyweight. The female then takes responsibility for the baby as the male heads towards the sea for food.

The Naked Mole Rat may not be the most attractive creature on the planet, but it is one of the most amazing, with fascinating superpowers. They rarely develop cancer and can live up to twenty-six years without ageing, far longer than most small animals. In addition, researchers have now discovered that they can survive eighteen minutes without oxygen.

Homo Sapiens, of course, are capable of withstanding great feats of endurance, whether it be flying through space, diving in the deepest ocean, or navigating the most hostile places on earth. Inspirational stories of man's ability to endure massive hardship, suffering and extreme trauma and injury are documented in the papers every day. From the battlefields of war, to the Paralympics, from the prisoner of war camps, to the base camps on Everest. Humankind epitomises true grit and staying power and that is why we are the most powerful and dangerous species on earth.

POWER POSES

Amy Cuddy, popular American social psychologist, author and lecturer, made us aware of the power of body language. In her hugely popular Ted talk, *Your Body Language May Shape Who You Are*, she states that our non-verbal language governs how other people think and feel about us. She also states that those people with a more open posture and mannerisms – which demonstrate confidence – will get the best jobs. Animals naturally use posturing to convey power and aggression by expanding their bodies. They expand to make themselves look bigger, more confident and more scary, and it works!

Your physicality will also help to influence the next two important concepts.

ESSENCE AND PRESENCE

These two are close allies, if you have ever met a celebrity in the normal world, were you surprised by their physical size? I know I have been. They always seem to be much smaller than you think they are going to be. However, their essence and presence is often jaw dropping and the energy they create is like a huge force field.

To demonstrate this point, I am keen to share this personal story with you. I was attending a two-day leadership course when someone walked into the room late. Myself and the rest of the attendees all registered an element of curiosity and mild surprise because it was at least 11am, on the first day of the course. The facilitator was also taken off-guard and showed mild signs of annoyance that the flow was interrupted by her entrance. "We have all introduced ourselves and explained our reasons for being on this course and what we are hoping to get out of this day. Could you please introduce yourself and your reason for being here?" He said in a clearly irritated way.

We were all wearing badges with our names on them and

possibly to give her a bit of support, I smiled warmly at the newcomer. However, her reply was unexpected.

In answer to the facilitator's question she replied, "My name is Alison Winch and I have come here today to meet Rosie Tomkins."

Intrigued and flattered, I couldn't wait for the coffee break. I was sure she had mixed me up with someone else because I had never seen her before.

As soon as the facilitator stopped for the break, I felt Alison's presence and essence powering across the room at me and as she walked across it got stronger.

"Rosie" she said, "are you interested in horses?"

Of all the questions she could have asked, I could not have imagined this was one of them.

I had recently sold my adventure sports company and was implementing a new product launch across forty-two health clubs nationwide and horses were not at the forefront of my mind. But I answered her honestly.

"Yes, I have always loved horses. Why do you ask?"

"Would you be prepared to join me in Northamptonshire for a business session working with horses?" replied Alison. Despite being taken completely unawares, because of the adventurer within me, I accepted her request.

And so it was that I arrived in Northamptonshire a few weeks later to spend a couple of hours face to face with an unknown horse. I was extremely sceptical about the possibilities that an animal was going to be able to help me with my business challenges. How wrong I was!

I was also arrogant in my assumption that I probably wouldn't learn anything. How wrong I was! I also assumed that this would be a session focusing on the soft side of business. How wrong I was yet again!

What happened in that couple of hours was transformational. For myself, for my business, and for my relationships with my employees. I learnt quickly and effectively what kind of leader I was and how that impacted on other people, sometimes positively, but also that I had a lot more to learn. This session did what no executive coaching session, management tool, or profiling tool could ever do, which was to maintain my attention in an experiential experience with another living creature – who had no interest in the outcome nor ego – and who responded to me only when I was authentic, aligned and congruent.

Little did I know that my session with Alison would change my life completely and that it would bring together aspects of myself, which I had been missing for a long time. However, I trusted that she had something unique and different to show me.

This was not any old horse that I was to work with. It was an Andalusian stallion; one and a half tonnes of rippling muscle, cheeky and curious. I was not going to be riding him, but working on the ground while he was at liberty. My only instruction from Alison was to find out his potential. I had no ropes, no collars, no saddles and no bridles. I was to find his potential in an open enclosure without riding him. But what happened was an extraordinary exploration of my own self, what I stood for and who I am as a person. I learnt more about myself in twenty minutes with that magnificent horse than I have learnt with any coach or consultant in my entire business life.

As I stood alone in the middle of an indoor arena with this magnificent specimen of a horse by my side, I decided that I had totally lost the plot. What was I doing? I had also found out a few days earlier that I was twelve weeks pregnant. What craziness was this? Every possible emotion passed through my mind, but I was here and he was waiting!

I could not connect with any form of verbal communication or logic. I had to come from somewhere else and dig deep inside myself to find out how I was going to get through the next twenty minutes and stay alive. Basically, I had to fall back to an intuitive state, as I couldn't use language – I had to demonstrate leadership in a different way. I had forgotten how powerful those concepts were until that experience with Alison.

I learnt more in that session – with that beautiful horse – than I could possibly have learnt anywhere else. It was nothing to do with horsemanship; it was to do with leadership.

- I learnt that I am a creative risk-taker who expects people to loyally follow, even when sometimes they are following blindly without any reassurance.

- I learnt that other people need a closer bond with me and they are not always happy at the pace I set. I need to watch my energy and monitor how appropriate it is for other people.

- I learnt to communicate my intentions clearly, so the people I work with feel included and safer.

- I learnt that I need to have much more trust in my team and to always have their back.

- I learnt about the positive attributes of my innate leadership style, but I also learnt about the shadow side of my leadership and how to temper this.

- I learnt that appreciation is far more important than incentives.

- I learnt that another living creature can mirror my actions and give me an extraordinary insight into a living business.

- I learnt humility.

This wonderful and insightful woman Alison – to whom I have dedicated this book – had given me a rare gift into a powerful way of being.

After the session, Alison confided in me that she had breast cancer and I confided in her that I was pregnant and separating from my husband. We met one more time when I went to see my horse partner – who had given me so much on that day – give a demonstration as part of the Equestrian Theatre at Earls Court in London. As you can imagine to see this proud animal demonstrating his full potential was humbling in the extreme.

After the birth of my son and my divorce, I was eager to reconnect with Alison and to progress this work into the business arena. I felt Alison symbolised the first runner in a relay team and she was passing the baton to me as the second runner. Three years had gone by and I felt ready to begin my journey into this work and was so looking forward to meeting her again. Sadly, that meeting never happened. Alison's journey was over, she died of breast cancer in 2005. She had already passed the baton to me and its flame burns deeply in my heart. My leg of the journey had begun.

What flame in another person, or other people, have you ignited?

CHAPTER 7

MARKING YOUR TERRITORY

I HAVE NEVER INTENDED TO SUGGEST that Natural Intelligence should be used without the other intelligences of IQ, EQ and SQ. It naturally seems to me that a balanced leadership should contain a form of physical intelligence, which I refer to as Natural Intelligence.

Natural Intelligence on its own could have disastrous outcomes; the reactive path is not always the best one to take. The gut feel has to be tempered with logical thought, otherwise we would never climb onto an aircraft, or set sail in a boat across an ocean. However, just as Natural Intelligence has to be tempered, so do the other forms of recognised intelligence.

NATURAL INTELLIGENCE ALONE IS NOT ENOUGH

On one of those early spring mornings when the ground is quite wet and there is a gentle mist rolling off the land, my daughter and I had tacked up the horses early and were looking forward to riding in the woods. We were on the rolling landscape of Exmoor.

Sheltered by the trees, we picked our way along some of the paths made by deer and badgers. The light filtered through the trees and it was magical. There was no need to say anything; there never is in these special moments in life. In fact, speaking would have disconnected us from the beauty we were privileged to be witnessing.

Suddenly a mewing sound became audible and as we continued down the leafy track, it came closer. The horses started to prance. They had picked up the energy of another creature and were transmitting their unease. As we came around the corner a small grey kitten was directly in our path. Without thinking, I quickly dismounted and scooped up the kitten before it could be trampled by our nervous horses. Stuffing it down the front of my jumper, I immediately remounted and we continued onwards.

After five or ten minutes I became transfixed by two extraordinary magnetic eyes, peering out from deep inside my V-neck jumper. Perplexed, I rode on, but with the slow dawning of something not being quite right.

I said to my daughter, "I'm not sure this is a kitten."

She replied jokingly, "Is it a hedgehog?"

"Very funny!" I said, but seriously I was questioning my

judgement because I no longer thought it was a kitten. Its eyes were so deeply slate blue and it felt wilder than wild. What colour are fox cubs? I thought to myself.

Reality started to kick in and the slow dawning of realization crept into my consciousness. I wasn't holding a kitten next to my breast I was harbouring a truly wild animal; a fox cub ... oh, yikes!

Fortunately, there was no harm done to either species. We returned to the spot where we had found the animal and I returned it to the wild and to a fate I had no hand in.

This true story reminds me on a regular basis, of what could happen if we only rely on Natural Intelligence.

It highlights how important it is to apply all the intelligences together, to make an informed decision before you take action.

However, the best outcome was the tremendous hilarity I caused the locals, when word got around about the latest exploits of the girl from London, literally embracing local wildlife!

HARD WIRED TO TERRITORY

In the wild, animals mark their territory for many reasons, using many different strategies and many different smells and odours. Why do they do this? Often it is a warning to keep out, but sometimes it is an invitation to come closer and breed. Territorial behaviour possesses several critical functions in the evolution and preservation of species. It has been suggested that territoriality serves the purposes of distributing or spreading animals across a large area, resulting in the proper use of feeding resources to enable safe and undisturbed breeding cycles. For example, in birds, territoriality ensures they do not build nests too close together. It is also said to reduce aggression in the animal species.

Humans mark territory physically with fences, walls, buildings, moats and lawyers. They defend their areas ferociously. Perhaps a more civilised way of interpreting this would be to look at boundaries. Everyone has boundaries; tangible boundaries and intangible ones. It is part and parcel of being an individual and your boundaries are attached strongly to your values. They are probably embedded deeply in our limbic system from early man.

For example, no one would take kindly to someone entering their home uninvited. In business we create brands, and trademark our goods and ideas, which is definitely a way of trying to protect our territory from those people who wish to constantly crash and pillage. Interestingly, open plan offices were constructed to encourage people to be more approachable and inclusive. Now most open plan offices have cubicles or obstacles erected to create personal space. Try changing seats after a coffee break to see how people react, or move closer to someone in a library and watch the other person's reaction.

Do you ever consider how important your boundaries are?

Sometimes, breaking through boundaries is used as a weapon. All major crimes have an invasion of personal space at their core, whether it be rape, murder, theft, violence or abuse of any kind. These actions cause the ultimate loss of power for the victim.

Loss of power – at any level – has a catastrophic effect on us, it causes us to waver in our self-belief and confidence; it can lead to serious illness and depression. It is important to safeguard against this or rebuild our boundaries as soon as possible.

One of the most common challenges I see when working with people, is how they have lost control of their boundaries. Once on a senior management course, a delegate believed that she always needed to say "yes" to any request from a senior colleague, resulting in a serious erosion of self-worth. Learning to say "no" at times has helped her mental well-being and to work more positively.

FLEXING OUR MUSCLES

How do we go about owning our own territory, flexing our muscles, both physically and intellectually? My belief is that you find your power, and once you have found it you stick to this influencing strategy; be a specialist rather than a generalist. There is real pressure in business to possess an assortment of skills and to have learning agility. However, I am not sure this is the best use of our time and expertise.

Do animals learn broad skills? Do lions attempt to fly or a naked mole rat adapt to living above ground? Of course, we need to be learning, growing and evolving all the time – but this is a steady evolution, not an overnight transformation.

"What is my job on the planet? What is it that needs doing, that I know something about, that probably won't happen unless I take responsibility for it?"

BUCKMINSTER FULLER

REAL PEOPLE, REAL LEARNING

I once worked with a well-known agency that specialised in creativity in business. This charismatic team was not only fun and inspirational but they already thought way outside the box. I felt I needed to challenge the team members in a very special way for them to get deep learning and insights from my leadership programme. I pulled out all the stops and created a unique challenge to hopefully stretch their abilities to the maximum.

As the day progressed and the challenges intensified, what happened was fascinating. This agency was brilliant at inspiring delegates and creating the 'Wow Factor' in business. However, outside its own environment and outside its normally extensive comfort zone, the confidence and power of intention was starting to unravel. Observation of the group showed that the gut feeling and body language was strong. However, underneath there was a certain amount of 'faking it' going on. When the participants were asked to reflect on this aspect of the programme, they replied that they didn't actually think the task was possible.

In stepped their office manager; this lady was responsible for making everything happen. Her job was to liaise with all the clients and make sure events ran smoothly and actually happened, on time and within budget. Physically, she was not out and about meeting the people, however she was a strong presence 'behind the scenes' of the business. She was a safe pair of hands.

To everyone's surprise, she attacked the challenge with a wonderful sense of 'this is going to happen', displaying confidence in her own ability. And, of course, she secured the positive result that everyone else had really struggled with.

She said afterwards, "When my CEO told me beforehand that we would be working with horses to find out our management attributes, I was extremely sceptical. Now that I have done it, I know it really works. You can feel and see it working. The learning is a much more tangible process. It is not just written words that go in one ear and out the other. It gave me a lasting memory and was really beneficial for the team because we have never had these discussions before and are now going to implement them on a regular basis. We weren't expecting miracles, but a miracle happened. It was a positive new step forward for our business."

INSTINCTIVE INSIGHTS

- You need to have all the intelligences informing your choices.

- The power of intention comes from the mind as well as the body; you need to be congruent throughout.

- When you are in a feeling state, it is difficult to retain information. When people are outside their comfort zone; sometimes they freeze. They may have insights into how their own clients may feel; valuable, new information to process when dealing with their clients in the future. They might access newfound respect for the different skills of their employees, which can be a memorable anchor for the future. People learn where their territory lies and how to stay within it. In the example above, the office manager owned her territory.

STANDING IN YOUR POWER AND KNOWING YOUR TERRITORY

Mfuwe Lodge in Zambia happens to have been built next to a mango tree that one family of wild elephants has always visited when the fruit ripens. When they returned one year and found that a new luxury accommodation hotel complex had been built in their way, how do you think they responded? Without damage or hurting anyone, they simply walked through the hotel reception, on their annual route to their kitchen larder, the mango tree.

""Power is not always about force and dominance, but a quiet intention to proceed towards our goal."

Andy Hogg, director at the Bushcamp Company that runs the Lodge, had lived in South Luangwa National Park since 1982 and said despite all his years of dealing with wild animals "he had never seen such intimate interaction between man and beast. This is the only place in the world where elephants freely get so close to humans.

"The elephants start coming through base camp in late November of each year to eat the mangos from our trees. When they are ripe the elephants come through and they stand about for four to six weeks coming back each day or second day to eat the mangos."

Living in the 5,000 square mile national park, the ten strong elephant herd is led to the Lodge each day by Wonky Tusk, an intrepid matriarch elephant who was named for her backward facing tusk.

This is a totally natural phenomenon. The elephants come here of their own accord and it is certainly a rare, but magnificent sight. The hotel is delighted with their new tourist attraction.

EROSION OF OUR SENSES

Why are we not concerned about the dulling of the senses? Take our sense of smell. According to scientists, modern life is ruining mankind's sense of smell. Our sense of smell is devolving and we should take this loss more seriously because it will have an impact on the future of all mankind and when lost it will be irreversible.

Why is it important? We can utilise other animals when necessary – for example, the use of sniffer dogs to find drugs and some cancers. However, they will not be able to protect us from food that has gone off, or smoke from a forest fire, or a gas leak. There is also the view that the lack of the sense of smell is contributing to obesity because people are preferring richer tasting food, loaded with extra salt, sugar and spice.

Our sense of smell is also linked to our libido. Smell is a form of communication between partners. Indeed, it may help determine the choice of partners. It also contributes to a 'feel good' factor; the smell of newly cut hay or grass, or the smell of white lilies.

WHEN WILL WE AWAKEN FROM OUR FOLLY?

As statistics go, Gallup Poll results are indicative of the views of many people. In recent years, when people have been asked what they are looking for in a leader, the results were nearly always courage, passion, inspiration and a sense of purpose. But in Gallup's most recent StrengthsFinder poll, the results had changed dramatically. Respondents now wanted a leader who provides stability, hope and shows compassion.

What leadership qualities are you looking for?

CHAPTER 8

AT LIBERTY

THE ALARM IS SOUNDING. If we continue to neglect our Natural Intelligence we will become dangerously unbalanced and we will no longer be safe custodians of our planet.

"Once nature determined how we survived. Now we determine how nature survives."

SIR DAVID ATTENBOROUGH

Looking back at our recent history, humans are the only species on earth who follow leaders displaying clear signs of being out of balance. Look at the leaders we are influenced by today. They may be great intellectual leaders; they may be powerful emotional leaders; or they may be charismatic spiritual or religious leaders; but are they balanced leaders? Truly liberated leaders?

All the chapters of this book are interwoven to position you as a liberated leader. With simple stories that signal profound insights, which slot together and can bring about a new paradigm in leadership to be more balance in the world. By understanding how all the intelligences link together, we can create more harmony in business and less stress and competition.

LIBERATED LEADERSHIP

Liberated leadership in the wild is an oxymoron. It is the only kind of leadership possible, so let's pay it some attention!

The premise so far is that everyone is a leader, that we all need to take responsibility; our masks need to be removed. You need to know why you are here, follow your heart; and remember you are not alone. You need to accept other people for who they are, be seen in the world, to lead people and make a difference in other people's lives. Accept what is, listen and create change. Realise that you have the power to choose what it is. When we do this our collective intelligence will strengthen and the feeling of being overwhelmed will diminish. We can fight to stop new ideas and initiatives being strangled by bureaucracy before they flourish. We can end the soul-destroying task of constant reporting that goes on in organisations. And we can expose the egos, on the rampage in many businesses, which do not serve anyone. Not a small proposition, but I know we can do it!

When I jointly set up my second company, it was a training business aimed at high level corporate women who wished to break through the glass ceiling into the boardroom. However, I realised early on there was a misconception that liberated leadership meant walking away from your existing job to some kind of cornucopia in the outside world.

If you can walk away, you already have freedom.

What perhaps needs liberating is our feeling of being caged by the five Fs: **futility; frustration; fear; lack of fulfilment; and faking it**. These feelings come from within us not from an external source. This is one of the hardest propositions to get across as a business coach and it is not easy to handle. Most people want to apportion blame to other people. Even when we can intellectually accept that these feelings are under our own control, it is difficult to change the mindset.

Below is a simple formula that has helped me greatly in my life. It is called ERO and it shows clearly how we have evolved to be able to pause and take stock of events before deciding on appropriate action. This uniquely sets us apart and possibly why we are the most successful animal that has ever lived.

ERO

EVENT → RESPONSE → OUTCOME

In short, neither animal nor man can control an event. However, man can pause before deciding which response is appropriate. Humans can also look forward to an outcome. What do I wish the end result to be? How can I behave to bring about this preferred outcome? Only then, when we have thought through the implications, do we act or choose a response. This is extremely valuable because we become familiar with choice. We are steering our life from the inside out and growth, for a leader, always starts from within.

The other wonderful trait that has assisted me on my journey to be the best liberated leader that I can be, comes from the work of Mike George, spiritual leader, author and motivational speaker. He coined the term 'detached observer', which allows us to witness an event without becoming emotionally affected. He believes we serve no-one if we are drawn into the emotion of any event. Animals seem to concur with this. As far as we know they don't have the emotional turmoil that we often experience at challenging times.

Compassion serves the world, but sympathy or pity don't. Humanity can be a driver for change whereas benevolence, not always. Self-confidence can serve, but ego can derail.

Being a 'detached observer' is a stabilising force in any business and will give employees a wonderful sense of security, which will develop into a crisis-proof enterprise.

"A liberated company is one that has achieved:

Freedom + Responsibility = Happiness + Performance"

ISSAC GETZ

DETACHED OBSERVER

It is relatively easy to lead when times are good and business is buoyant. However, it takes a certain kind of leader to deal with crisis and turbulent times. Those leaders dealing with life and death situations on a regular basis have to dig very deep to stay detached. Imagine being a doctor in the middle of a bloody battlefield or in an Accident and Emergency Unit after a bomb atrocity. Imagine leading a team fighting to prevent child trafficking or trying to prosecute someone for gross negligence with animals. Or being a war correspondent seeing first hand man's inhumanity to man.

This is the shadow side of leadership; the long dark night of the soul. And for me, this is the ultimate test of centred and liberated leadership. Can I stay calm while all around me there is chaos and despair?

What kind of person am I under pressure? And can I accept that person?

The famous and wonderful poem by Rudyard Kipling sums up the detached observer. Although, in the last line I want to change the word from 'man' to 'leader'.

IF

"If you can keep your head when all about you;
Are losing theirs and blaming it on you,
If you can trust yourself when all men doubt you,
But make allowance for their doubting too.
If you can wait and not be tired by waiting,
Or being lied about, don't deal in lies,
Or being hated, don't give way to hating,
And yet don't look too good, nor talk too wise:

If you can dream - and not make dreams your master;
If you can think - and not make thoughts your aim;
If you can meet with Triumph and Disaster,
And treat those two impostors just the same;
If you can bear to hear the truth you've spoken
Twisted by knaves to make a trap for fools,
Or watch the things you gave your life to, broken,

And stoop and build 'em up with worn-out tools:

If you can make a heap of all your winnings
And risk it on one turn of pitch-and-toss,
And lose, and start again at your beginnings
And never breathe a word about your loss;
If you can force your heart and nerve and sinew
To serve your turn long after they are gone,
And so hold on when there is nothing in you
Except the Will which says to them: "Hold on!"

If you can talk with crowds and keep your virtue,
Or walk with Kings - nor lose the common touch,
If neither foes nor loving friends can hurt you,
If all men count with you, but none too much;
If you can fill the unforgiving minute
With sixty seconds' worth of distance run,
Yours is the Earth and everything that's in it,
And - which is more - you'll be a Man, my son!"

RUDYARD KIPLING

TOUGH LEADERSHIP

Can I serve the situation without becoming emotionally involved? Can I get the job done to the best of my ability without becoming attached to the outcome?

These are deep and difficult questions. Of course if I can't, I shouldn't be leading. I need to be detached to be able to choose the right outcome; otherwise I am not engaging all my intelligences and monumental mistakes can be made.

Many people like to imagine that nature is soft and fluffy. They see the idyllic farm set amid the magnificent landscape of rolling hills, the sun-drenched valleys, sleepy cottage gardens and honeysuckle around the door. The farm animals graze quietly in the pasture and everything seems in harmony. However, as always there is a shadow side. As nightfall begins so does the killing. Many animals hunt at night; newborn lambs can be snatched by a hungry fox, the owls swoop down on unsuspecting mice, badgers mercilessly killing inside the hen house and cats preying on any living creature that moves. Rabbits are picked off by predators as they eat grass under the stars. It is not Beatrix Potter; nature is not soft and fluffy. While the farmhouse snoozes safely through the night, carnage is going on outside.

EXPOSING THE UNDERBELLY

Although leadership sometimes takes great courage both in business and often in our home life as well, what does tough leadership mean "Perfect Leadership" is there such a thing as a perfect leader or a perfect partner?

Of course not and how much time effort and stress go into trying to fulfil this fallacy? The pressure to have all the answers , to lead the way, to not show weakness takes a heavy toll and is inhuman.

According to a recent Equilar study the average tenure of a CEO is 5 years.

When animals play we know it is a form of preparation for what lies ahead. They are acquiring life skills that will serve them as adults and they enter maturity. When the play gets too rough, an animal will surrender by rolling on its back, so that its neck and underbelly are exposed – it is an act of total vulnerability – and it will live to fight another day.

For some reason humans have become hardwired to NOT show their throat or soft underbelly at any cost. We feel that whatever the circumstance we have to stay strong, all knowing, decisive, always the top dog, it's exhausting!

This hereditary response no longer serves us in our man-made jungle. If we could expose our underbelly we might be able to design a new imperfect leadership style that lasts a lifetime rather than a few years. An imperfect leadership which acknowledges that one person cannot have a complete set of skills.

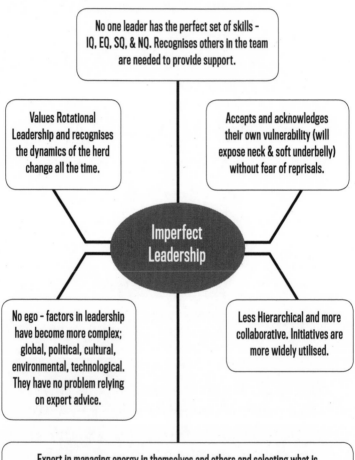

No one leader has the perfect set of skills - IQ, EQ, SQ, & NQ. Recognises others in the team are needed to provide support.

Values Rotational Leadership and recognises the dynamics of the herd change all the time.

Accepts and acknowledges their own vulnerability (will expose neck & soft underbelly) without fear of reprisals.

Imperfect Leadership

No ego - factors in leadership have become more complex; global, political, cultural, environmental, technological. They have no problem relying on expert advice.

Less Hierarchical and more collaborative. Initiatives are more widely utilised.

Expert in managing energy in themselves and others and selecting what is appropriate right now for the business. Understands that front end, driving, motivational, inspirational energy cannot be sustained for long periods without fatigue.

CAN ANIMALS PUSH THE PAUSE BUTTON?

Consider this online news story about Russian dogs written by Cheyenne Macdonald for the *dailymail.com:*

> ## "Moscow's 'metro dogs' have learned to navigate the city's subways: canine senses help them master complex routes, claims scientist."

"There are roughly 35,000 stray dogs in Moscow and about twenty of them have become regular commuters on the metro. These dogs haven't found themselves on the train by accident," explained Jacqueline Boyd of Nottingham Trent University in an article for *The Conversation.* "This unusual behaviour is likely attributed to a combination of factors, from the co-evolution of humans and our canine companions, to their fine-tuned sensory capabilities. Over many years of coexistence, dogs have learned to recognize and respond to human signals," Boyd explains. "As humans have learned to cope with a changing environment, dogs may have too. These social skills strongly suggest a degree of convergent evolution between dogs and humans," Boyd writes. "This occurs when different species evolve similar traits while adapting to a shared environment. The abilities of the metro dogs might suggest they have developed coping mechanisms similar to those of their fellow human commuters."

How do they do it? Andrei Neuronov another animal behavioural expert, told the *New Yorker* that dogs have learned to recognise station names, much as many dogs can recognise short commands and their own names. But this ability is used to different ends by different metro dog tribes. There are three models of metro dogs, he explained: dogs who live in the subway but do not travel; dogs who use the subway to travel short distances instead of walking; and entrepreneurial dogs who spend the day riding back and forth, busking. This last type of dog takes long trips, working the crowd for treats and emotional contact."

Does this equate to animals evolving to push the pause button? Do these dogs actually work out where they want to go on the metro and respond accordingly? Or are they following their instinct?

Well if they can, how about you? Push that pause button now and make a personal choice. "Am I in a cage or a safe place?"

As a liberated leader, you influence other people to be who they are, to find their own path and to have the confidence to try.

REAL PEOPLE, REAL LEARNING

Often when working with a senior management team, they describe my work as a disruptive experience. They come because their intention is to shake things up, challenge and have honest conversations that have been avoided in the past.

One particular team were no different. On paper they boasted a formidable repertoire of IQ skills and attributes. However, as they were a new team coming together, my brief was to build trust quickly, to provide an experience of supporting each other, and to give them permission to challenge or break the rules if they were no longer serving the organisation.

Part of the day's training was going to be outside in nature, which they were not told about until the night before. The challenge was for the team to meet with a herd of horses and persuade one of them to make a small jump without touching the animals in any way and without riding the horse in question. The only piece of equipment they had was a bucket of water.

The rules were very basic. Stay connected physically as a team unless you are leading. Only the leader (who is detached from the group) can speak. But you can rotate the leadership as often as necessary to get the job done.

This experiential learning experience tested the group on a number of levels:

STRATEGICALLY; how to deal with the unknown. None of the team members had any previous knowledge or experience with horses.

ASSUMPTION; that the water had some relevance to the successful outcome of the task.

ENERGETICALLY; how did they nominate the leader? What did it feel like to fail? How supportive were the group? How did it feel to have shared responsibility and rotational leadership?

CREATIVELY: How much help or what resources did they request from the environment or how did they change the environment to assist them? Did they ask for help outside the group?

INDEPENDENTLY: At what point did they challenge the rules or the instructions?

INTENTIONALLY; Did the whole group believe the task was possible? How easy was it to trust each other's methods and to follow someone else?

"On this course, we learnt so much about our own, as well as other people's, strengths and weaknesses. Watching the people you work with doing the exercises and how they dealt with each situation was very powerful for us all. Each person gained a sense of identity and embraced their innate capabilities. We learnt that you can push through using Natural Intelligence, and we can take that into the workplace to succeed at whatever we do."

The multiplier effect for this team was that the bonding, trust building and respect for each other's skills was fast-tracked. This new team quickly felt comfortable with each other, winning new contracts and becoming the highest performing team in their sector.

INSTINCTIVE INSIGHTS

The list of insights, which this team learnt as a result of this training experience, was extensive. Their debrief comments were highly memorable and immediately applicable:

- To understand liberated leadership is to understand a context of no ego.

- When I don't have the answers, is someone else more equipped to deal with this situation than me?

- How reassuring it was to have rotational leadership. The team will get the result by pooling their skills for the good of the whole.

- The support of the team was invaluable when things don't work out.

- We challenged ourselves afterwards and asked: Why did it take so long to put down the bucket? Are we carrying old thinking that once served a purpose, but doesn't serve us anymore? Interestingly, this learning came because we thought about a dog with a stick. They do not carry objects for very long if they are not using them for a valuable purpose.

- This exercise with the horses made us ask questions: How do we take care of teammates; do we have their back?

- We learnt about what it felt like to follow and not always lead.

- We understood – eventually – where the energy was in the group and to question if it was appropriate at that moment for that task.

What are you carrying in your life that no longer serves you?

CHAPTER 9

PANNING FOR GOLD

SIR KENNETH ROBINSON, is an internationally recognised leader in the development of creativity, innovation and human potential, and is also famous for his views on education. He said, "Everyone is born with exceptional talents and we squander them pretty ruthlessly ... creativity is as important in education as literacy and we should treat it with the same status. "

CREATIVITY

When I talk about panning for gold it is not a financial material, money or wealth. Gold here is about your talents and creativity. For a literary agent gold is a bestselling book. Gold for a doctor is saving someone's life. Gold for a comedian is making someone laugh.

"Why fit in, when you were born to stand out?"

DR ZEUS

When we are born we all have something priceless in our DNA and it is our job to find it and be true to it. These small golden nuggets can be covered up by masses of external factors: education, peer group pressure, expectations, financial need, desire to conform and more. Whatever it is, we need to pan for our hidden gold and benefit from its value once we have identified what it is and accessed it.

"Don't die with your music still inside you."

DR WAYNE DYER

PROTECT YOUR GOLD

In business, gold is often defined by your brand and too often we see the integrity of the brand being damaged by overzealous growth plans or expansion into new markets, which do not serve the customer. Sometimes it might make sense to freeze, stay small, be niche and protect our gold.

This is beautifully demonstrated in this well-known story.

There was once a businessman who was sitting by the beach in a small Brazilian village. As he sat there, he saw a Brazilian fisherman rowing a small boat towards the shore having caught quite a few big fish.

The businessman was impressed and asked the fisherman, "How long does it take you to catch so many fish?"

The fisherman replied, "Oh, only a short while."

"Then, why don't you stay longer at sea and catch even more?" The businessman was astonished.

"This is enough to feed my whole family," the fisherman said.

The businessman asked, "What do you do for the rest of the day?"

The fisherman replied, "Well, I usually wake up early in the morning, go out to sea and catch a few fish, then go back and play with my kids. In the afternoon, I take a nap with my wife and when evening comes, I join my buddies in the village for a drink. We play guitar, sing and dance throughout the night."

The businessman offered a suggestion to the fisherman.

"I have a PhD in business management. I can help you to become a more successful person. From now on, you should spend more time at sea and try to catch as many fish as possible. When you have saved enough money, you could buy a bigger boat and catch even more fish. Soon you will be able to afford to buy more boats, set up your own company, your own production plant for canned seafood and your own product distribution network. By then, you will have moved out of this village and to Sao Paulo, where you can set up your company's headquarters to manage your other branches."

The fisherman asked the businessman, "And after that?"

The businessman laughed heartily, "After that, you can live like a king in your own house and when the time is right, you can go public and float your shares on the Stock Exchange and you will be rich."

The fisherman asked again, "And after that?"

The businessman said, "After that, you can finally retire, you can move to a house by the fishing village, wake up early in the morning, catch a few fish, then return home to play with kids, have a nice afternoon nap with your wife and when evening comes, you can join your buddies for a drink, play the guitar, sing and dance throughout the night!"

The fisherman was puzzled, "Isn't that what I am doing now?"

The fisherman had already found his gold.

DIFFERENT VERSIONS OF SUCCESS

Earlier, I referred to the natural fight, flight or freeze response in (Chapter 1), but for a hare its survival success depends on a combination of skills. The ability to run at high speed, to camouflage itself and to freeze. Without a burrow, lair, or den the hare is exposed and when death or danger is imminent, they use their golden nuggets to stay still, crouched down with their ears flat back, disappearing into the landscape. It is an effective strategy for success.

Perhaps the learning in business is that pushing the stop button to pause, reflect and reconsider may become a useful strategy for survival. It is time to go on that treasure hunt and uncover your personal gold.

WHAT WAS JACK'S GOLD AND WHERE DID IT TAKE HIM?

This is the part of the story book where normally you expect to read an inspirational success story about how Jack became a hugely successful international polo player on the glittering worldwide circuit, with a six-figure salary, fashion models on his arm and a five-star celebrity lifestyle.

However, success for Jack does not encompass those material possessions and behaviours. Jack lives on his terms. This is the boy who when he left school his parting gift was to fill the playground with sheep, to demonstrate that he was not a follower. At fifteen years of age his message was clear. I will not be herded by you or anyone.

His gold is different to many other people and he remains an untamed spirit.

I was lucky enough to meet jack and to see him play polo as well as watch him live his life. Most polo matches are uneventful; however, one day there was a horrific accident on the polo pitch. A horse had a heart attack during an important match and the rider, a young girl called Elly was trapped beneath the tangle of horseflesh. As the crowd held its collective breath and every parent felt that cold realisation of catastrophe, Elly appeared like magic from underneath the horse and luckily was completely unharmed.

Many years later we were travelling back from a skiing holiday together and Elly shared with me how she had felt at that moment, trapped and alone, fearing the worst underneath one and half tonnes of horse flesh. In those intense moments when her life was in the balance, she was unaware that Jack was at her side. He had dismounted in seconds and risking his own life, pulled her clear. Elly had experienced – first hand – that exquisite feeling of having a hand on your back! Jack's Natural Intelligence saved her life. Within seconds she could have been crushed by the weight of the dead horse. What is strange now, so long after the event, is that no one acknowledged his courageous act and Jack himself would not have wanted any accolade.

We love to hear people's 'rags to riches' stories where things turn out in multicolour splendour; where the hero walks away with his prize. However, Jack used his gold to weave a life which gave him purpose, passion and contentment.

I have seen Jack ride horses other people would or could not get close to. His connection with nature is so in tune that once on their backs he becomes at one with the horse; fearless, connected and a calming influence. He has always been able to transform the energy of the horse into a formidable force on the polo pitch. I have seen him achieve this with my own eyes many times – both horse and rider in complete natural flow, with a combined intention and energy.

He used this remarkable skill to carve out a decent living for himself and when his international playing days were over he transferred his skill into mentoring other people. Happily married into a racing empire and managing a polo club and the estate, he now has children of his own who are learning first-hand the language of animals and nature.

What is your gold, and how will you use it for the benefit of the whole?

REAL PEOPLE, REAL LEARNING

I visited Ireland recently to work with students attending a leadership program. The mature students came from many diverse backgrounds and had many valuable insights to share with each other. The first group was no exception; diverse backgrounds is an understatement. The group consisted of: a governor from an open prison, aeronautical engineer, fashion designer, firefighter, head teacher, secretary and ex-curling world champion. This group had been struggling with a collaborative project and the tutor mentioned they were not gelling as a group. There was friction and a lack of respect clearly evident when I met them on the first day.

As the day progressed, I saw an opportunity to 'pan for gold', to uncover each student's golden nuggets in front of the team and see the changing perspectives as respect started to slowly emerge. During the first challenge, I asked all of them to partner up and to make a decision as to who was to be the leader and who would be the follower. After considerable debate they arrived at their decisions.

First up was the fashion designer and the fireman. Predictably, the fireman had chosen to lead and the fashion designer was happy to follow. I quickly reversed the decision, so each of the delegates could benefit from a new perspective and possibly be slightly outside their comfort zone. So, the fashion designer became the leader and the fireman became the follower and had to wear a blindfold. This particular challenge I set was relatively simple, but the outcome surprised both myself and the observers!

The task was set and the fashion designer was given the freedom to be as creative as he desired as long as he kept his partner safe. And creative he was!

It was wonderful to watch the designer create a completely different way of achieving the result required. He was in his element, breaking the rules if they didn't serve him, changing the format and challenging the direction that other people may have taken. He worked as one with the horse and completed the task with fluidity and flair.

Meanwhile his partner was resistant, frustrated and upset. He stated that he felt out of control and completely disempowered.

The power of this situation was that both the designer and the fireman had to contemplate the appropriateness of their actions. Afterwards, they understood they had a responsibility as leaders to have the courage to step up and articulate when they are outside their comfort zone.

The designer said; "For the first time, I felt liberated to

trust my instinct and create something different, without fear of not following conventional patterns."

The fireman said; "Although this was truly uncomfortable, it taught me to value individuals who are coming from a different place to me. I realised afterwards that I should have spoken up earlier and expressed my unease. In my work role, it cemented my approach to act quickly, efficiently and effectively to save lives. Also, it will help me in the future to voice any concerns before it is too late."

INSTINCTIVE INSIGHTS

- Sometimes, when you are a leader it is hard to be a follower.

- Understanding what is appropriate in the present moment for each situation. If the fireman had been rescuing people from a burning building, it would be appropriate for a controlling, fast, effective and safe leadership style.

- Do you need to be controlling, fast, effective and safe?

- Do youn need to explore new territory, be creative, and follow your own path?

- How does trust impact the task you are trying to achieve?

- How do we build trust?

- Understanding and respecting other people's skills and essence; their personal gold.

- If you are not feeling safe or empowered, it is your responsibility to speak up and challenge the status quo.

CHAPTER 10

FLEX YOUR MUSCLES

"A formidable foe challenges the world today. It saps the economy of £400 billion in lost productivity. This foe is not the national defense budget, nor the cost of saving the environment. It is disengagement."

LISSA POHL

DISENGAGEMENT

Loss of momentum is contagious; people today want to feel they have a purpose and their work matters. Any form of disengagement or lack of ownership costs the company a fortune in output, recruitment, sales and loss of potential. When you are first recruited for your role in any organisation you are 'cock-a-hoop' – you bring passion, positivity and performance over and above what is expected of you, and this is termed the *discretionary effort*. It is what determines whether a company is good or great.

With disengagement comes a feeling of being unappreciated and a loss of personal power. Despite efforts by leadership trainers and consultants to value intellectual diversity – to inspire and to manage change – we are unable to impact and head off this pervasive modern trend. Disengagement affects around seventy percent of our workforce according to recent Gallup research.

OVER-COMPLICATION

Are we over-complicating everything? Can we simplify our very complex lives? When we over-complicate life and we do not use our own power, things start to slide and it is easy to become despondent and overwhelmed. I often work with groups of elite sportsmen and women, who have every expert encouraging them and searching for that important marginal gain, which will take them into a winning position.

Actually, it is often their lack of awareness of how their behaviour impacts other people which can cause so much angst. Once angst sets in, confidence is eroded swiftly and disengagement follows. Often, we concentrate on our own ego instead of the team requirements. But our human ways of gaining power and status are polar opposite to those in nature. Money, job title, achievements, sex, and fame are often the goals that humans seek. Whereas, in the wild, discipline, purpose, adaption, responsibility and struggle bond the herds and packs together. Respect is earned and disengagement means certain death.

When you work with horses, if they are not all working together for the good of the whole there is chaos. All social animals need structure and some type of leadership, or lives dissolve into chaos. Horses know – instinctively – that they have to bring all their skills to the table to survive. In the wild there is an alpha male and an alpha female responsible for the safety and direction of the herd. The other herd members will include sentinels who pick up danger on the horizon; socialisers who look after the youngsters; brood mares; those who can find water or minerals; and other horses that will fight off predators. They all have a role in the herd. They contribute to the success and their contribution may be the difference between making it through a harsh winter without starving or dying. They need their herd to be healthy and balanced, concentrating on the outcome of the whole.

Often the pressure on teams is so great, they are not concentrating on the outcome for the whole because they are so worried about their own personal performance. They are fearful of making a mistake, of not being good enough, of losing their jobs and facing professional failure. Their allegiance and their loyalty is not really secure. They can be performing for the good of themselves – instead of the good of the team – and that can be really obvious to everyone. Though we rarely articulate it, again because of fear! For the horses to be around this incongruency sends off a 'distress flare' and they react with honesty and immediately flag up that something is not right. You cannot trick them. Animals do not lie.

Nearly all animals, without signing a contract, simply – with no complication – commit to the herd, commit to the pack, commit to the flock and commit to being a part of something. This commitment is everywhere in nature and yet as a species the human race seems to be scared of commitment. We are becoming a race of people who do not really need to commit.

- Why do it?
- Why be bothered?

It is interesting that we tend to admire other people who are committed to causes. We look up to people such as Gandhi, Mother Teresa, George Washington, Martin Luther King, Rosa Parks, Florence Nightingale and Barrack Obama. People like David Attenborough and his commitment to nature. We really admire these people and yet we do not in ourselves often commit to building our lives around causes we believe in.

Commitment and trust are massive when you build a leadership team. When you are all bringing the best you can be to the table for the good of everyone. Even if it is for a short time, it feels good and the memory of it stays a lifetime. Remember when you scored the winning goal in that tournament. Remember when you won that first big client or contract. Remember, how against all odds you pulled it off!

If you are a team of doctors and you are working together on an operation, you are trusting everyone is doing their utmost to save the life of the patient. You have the same in business. When you are in a business with other people whom you care about, you are working together to be the best you can be for everyone, not merely for yourself.

It is really important that people feel committed and part of making a difference and they trust the other people around them are doing the same. They have to work together. They are no good on their own, hanging on to their individual patterns of behaviour. They say that geese are seventy percent more efficient when they fly as a flock than when flying alone (National Geographic, 2016).

"The whole is greater than the sum of its parts."

ARISTOTLE

We know the acronym for the word **TEAM** is 'Together Everyone Achieves More'.

When I work with groups, often their power of intention is not really present. They are faking it, simply going through the motions, and horses pick up on that very quickly. For example, if there are delegates trying to perform a task and there is no real power of intention, the horse can read it and will not co-operate. The minute they feel incongruities they become willful. They will turn away, assert their authority; they have lost trust in our judgement. Once animals are not tethered or confined, they will utilise their own Natural Intelligence to survive.

During the fatal Asian Tsunami in 2004, animals had picked up signs well before the disaster hit and they had moved to higher ground. Even the elephants tethered near the beach escaped by ripping up their posts to flee the danger. Incongruency means danger to any animal and we should heed the warning despite being the most intelligent species on earth. If we override these signals, we put ourselves in grave peril.

HOW DOES THIS IMPACT BUSINESS?

Unless the group comes together with a joint purpose, combining their skills to achieve a goal together without any incongruency, you will get a dismal result. As soon as there is disengagement it is like a virus that will sweep everyone up in its path. It can often start with one or two dissatisfied employees, but quickly infects the morale of everyone. Once it exists it is very difficult to redress the balance.

"All animals need some sort of purpose to be psychologically healthy."

CAESAR MILAN

Many international experts on leadership and human performance, use work with meditation to increase people's awareness of what is going on in their body and use breathing to return people to a state of calm. Wonderful work, but scientists have now proven that being around animals brings you back into this calm state very quickly and this is one of the reasons why leadership work with horses is on the increase.

When people are around horses, physiological changes take place. They connect with their electromagnetic field and rapid changes in hormones, testosterone, cortisol etc. can be detected. A horse's heart is hugely bigger than a human heart, and we are pulled into their electromagnetic field. Once you are in this electromagnetic field it affects your heart pattern and your hormones.

One of the unique differences with horses is that although they are a prey animal, they have this incredible ability to want to serve. Whereas if you were working with deer or sheep or zebras they would run away. Although humans inflict huge brutality and hardship on horses, they are literally man's best friend. They want to be beside us, they want to help and serve us in some way.

OWNERSHIP

Taking back control of our own destiny, the ability to respond and take responsibility have never been so needed as in our 21st century.

A key learning in life is that we all have habits, which can cause a positive or negative impact on our own life or the people around us. We all have patterns of behaviour and blind spots that we are not always aware of.

Unless you are prepared to expose yourself to a memorable experiential learning situation, you will continue to propagate those behaviours over and over again. Working in an experiential way makes you own up to your impact in the world. There can be no finger pointing and no blame; the buck stops with you. When the effect of your blind spots, your habits and your patterns show up and they are mirrored by a living organism like a horse or a dog in a powerful but non-threatening way, you then own your behaviour. You have the choice; does this way of being serve me?

The power of ownership extends to all areas of your life; what you eat, how you behave, and the quality of your relationships. This self-regulating mechanism allows you to make the right decisions for you.

It is fascinating that we very rarely see a fat animal in the wild because animals self-regulate. If they are left alone and they have no fear of drought or famine, they do a great job of keeping themselves in shape. And they need to be in shape because at any stage they are going to need to use their body to run away or to fight or to defend themselves. The only reason animals become fat is when they are under stress or lack fear.

For example, there are squirrels in England's national parks who are getting fat because humans are giving them food. Apparently, the confused squirrels believe they are heading for a famine and so they are stockpiling food in their bodies to get through. But they have actually given away their ownership and their ability to instinctively self-regulate and this has caused this unnatural problem.

It is the same with domesticated cats or dogs who we provide food for. I never give my puppy set meal times. Can you imagine how desperate pets get, when they are dependent on humans providing food and we get home late! I simply give my dog a bowl of food and he self-regulates. He doesn't eat too much. He doesn't get into a panic that his food will never be there. He knows he can eat when he wants to.

It is similar to staying in your personal power. Once you know who you are, what you stand for and what behaviour you own that serves you, it gives you confidence to take risks. Whatever happens you will have the tools to enable you to handle what comes up. More than that, it gives you an ability to step outside of your comfort zone; try something new, be fearless and creative.

Someone such as Steve Jobs, the late CEO of Apple, had strong beliefs around ownership. He believed there was no saying "no" – he would instruct his employees to find a way to innovate and to find an answer. In so doing, he built a workforce prepared to fail as well as prepared to step up and get things wrong. They weren't in any way penalized for these ideas, even though they might not to work. He encouraged growth and he encouraged people to step outside their comfort zone and embrace it.

The rest is history, Apple became one of the most innovative companies in the world. He empowered the people around him. However, more often than not, people have been disempowered from being who they are and bringing their best game to the table.

It is about having the confidence to own who you are.

These are the building blocks of confidence: knowing who you are; what you stand for; what your strengths are; when to collaborate; when to bring other people in to help you; knowing you need to take risks; when you need to step outside; when you need to make things happen; and that it will be okay.

As I say, we all have more than 400,000 years of DNA leadership in our genetic makeup. This is the reason we are on the planet today. We are leaders, all of us, and everything will be okay. We simply need to have trust, commitment and ownership of our lives.

I believe the reasons nature wildlife programmes are so popular is because they are almost calling us back to what we once were. Nature gives us great comfort, which is missing from our daily lives. These programmes represent the 'real' and instinctive, but critically they return us to the basics, the things that really matter. It is such a relief to watch these programmes and restore parts of our lives that we only glimpse as we rush at break neck speed to our next appointment. We are drawn to nature – not for our health but because it is an escape from the human anthill. Escape from our own competition and our own dramas.

It's your life

The wilderness and the corporate world have many

similarities. It is highly beneficial for the corporate world to learn from nature. In some areas, such as product engineering and medicine, it is already happening, but in terms of personal leadership and team leadership, this opportunity has not been developed until now! Nature demonstrates powerful lessons when we simply stop, observe and listen. Animals don't need man, but we need them.

As I bring this book to a close, I trust I have stimulated several new thought processes for you.

My aim is to introduce Natural Intelligence to the business community. To emphasise what powerful experiential learning can deliver for personal and professional leadership. To transform leadership training so Natural Intelligence – NQ – is always included alongside IQ, EQ and SQ.

To remind us that 'we are animals' and we need to take care of each other, to support each other, to feel that strong hand on our back, to trust other people, and to act for the good of the whole.

IN BALANCE, IN HARMONY

If you visit any watering hole in Africa during the abundant periods you will see zebras grazing among lions; gazelle alongside buffalo and giraffe; all different, all happily co-existing. In balance and in harmony. We have so much to learn from them. The answer to most of life's challenges is out there in nature.

As technology speeds up I have noticed that we are becoming more and more detached from nature. This lack of a natural anchor, especially for the younger generation, worries me greatly. These young people are the next leaders of the world as we know it. Are we equipping them with the relevant tools and mindset to steer a course where the world can prosper? There are more suicides in young men in their twenties and thirties than ever before. There is so much pressure on body image, sexual orientation, friendship groups, career success, money and material goods. There is a constant concern that they are missing out and that everyone is happily pursuing exciting pursuits – all accentuated by social media. There is even an anxiety called FOMO; the fear of missing out syndrome. Nobody wants to admit to failure, problems, boredom, or loneliness on social media. We feel pressured to portray a life well-lived, exactly like all the celebrities we see portraying the perfect life. It is not real life and in fact, isolation ensues.

Are we on a trajectory that will mean losing the ability to really connect? Could this disconnection be causing a form of acute loneliness that is new to our world?

As we come to the end of this book, I also hope that you are bringing in your own personal harvest – for yourself and your business.

It is not about ego; your place should be about gratitude, celebration and wanting to serve other people with confidence. You are energised, happy, in the zone, balanced and fearless. You are following your own personal compass to guide you. You are not listening to other people and what they think of you and what they think you should do. You are making a blueprint of your life. You are in harmony and in balance.

In the wild, there are many amazing examples of synergy and many animals spend the majority of their time in a place of peace. And when they do have to act, they often act together in a uniform way. There is no infighting, no ego, no competition; they simply get the job done.

You are your own gatekeeper. You are free to contribute to the world the work that you were born to do, and you will know this place when you arrive. It is a unique place and special because it will be effortless.

Leadership in the wild is not about position, it is about behaviour. Each herd or pack member contributes their skill for the good of the whole. And to emulate this liberated leadership in our world requires belief, trust and courage.

It is not the leadership of control, but the leadership of freedom. Natural Intelligence is about being a liberated leader.

Give yourself the permission to be the best liberated leader you can be and bring in a bountiful harvest.

To end, I share with you this beautiful poem, which my friend Alison loved so much.

I WILL NOT DIE AN UNLIVED LIFE

"I will not die an unlived life
I will not live in fear of falling
Or catching fire
I choose to inhabit my days
To allow my living to open me
To make me less afraid
More accessible
To loosen my heart
Until it becomes a wing
A torch, a promise

I choose to risk my significance
To live

So that which came to me as seed
Goes to the next as blossom
And what came to me
As blossom
Goes on as fruit."

DR DAWNA MARKOVA

What insights have you learnt from nature that will grow, empower and improve your leadership? Access your individual Natural Intelligence to make you a liberated leader for the future.

In the words of Dewitt Jones, National Geographic photographer: "Nature is a source of incredible energy, endless possibilities, and abundance of answers. Celebration is everywhere. Against all odds nature persists. Man is not separate from nature."

This book provides you with memorable anchors to nourish your personal leadership journey. You will have been drawn to different stories and they will have impacted you in myriad ways. When life rocks your foundation, remember these; and let them give you the confidence to endure.

Here are those key anchors.

LEADERSHIP – personal power and intention – the eyes of the Jaguar.

ENERGY – what energy is appropriate right now – the wild duck's expertise to achieve her goal. The cheetah always leaving something in the tank to protect itself from danger.

CONNECTION – beauty and coherence everywhere in the world – the unbelievable waggle dance of the bees.

COURAGE – to know your value and to live it – hummingbirds nesting in the trees with hawks.

OWNERSHIP – adapt or die – the Moscow metro dogs.

ACKNOWLEDGEMENTS

My greatest thanks to all animals, especially the horses; the grandmasters of authenticity. There is so much we can learn from these magnificent creatures on our planet. Without them this work could not happen.

For all the humans who had a hand on my back during the process of writing this book and beyond.

Thank you from my heart x

ABOUT THE AUTHOR

Rosie Tomkins is the founder of N-sinctive and Natural Capital Consultants Limited in the United Kingdom. She is a dedicated and passionate business entrepreneur, management consultant and sportswoman. She started her own lifestyle company more than thirty years ago, which she successfully led as managing director for more than ten years. Her first business offered adventure, sporting breaks and specialist holidays to high worth individuals and corporate clients.

Rosie researched and proactively targeted likely buyers, with the positive outcome of negotiating the sale of her business to one of the United Kingdom's fastest moving and dynamic PLCs. She was subsequently invited to join the board of directors and launched an innovative range of products nationwide to more than 120,000 members across forty-two health clubs.

Throughout her busy career, Rosie has amassed a comprehensive knowledge of learning philosophers and technologies, as well as experiencing their practical implication.

Her clients range from elite sports teams, pharmaceutical companies, engineering, education, airlines, to high end startup teams.

High performing teams and individuals benefit from her deep wisdom and her gift of making the insights and learning immediately relevant and applicable to any scenario in business or life.

Pioneering this work with teams in the United States and Europe, establishing a robust training program and leadership think tank, are among her next objectives.

Rosie lives on a farm near Bath in the West Country with her partner Paul and her youngest son Seb, three wonderful horses, one energetic dog and a feral, but friendly cat.

CONTACT ROSIE TOMKINS

EMAIL: rosie@n-stinctive.com

WEBSITE: www.n-stinctive.com

LINKEDIN: Rosie Tomkins

INSTAGRAM: @nstinctiveintelligence

TWITTER: @n_stinctive

YOUTUBE: Rosie Tomkins

FACEBOOK: www.facebook.com/N-stinctive-326422628074170

CLIENT TESTIMONIALS

"Rosie Tomkins and I worked together for a number of years running a small business that she had set up. I worked with her again because she designed and ran a development day, with horses, for the Global leadership team of my consultancy business. The day was a big success; it helped surface and shift some of the systemic patterns, as well as providing a rich experience for personal learning. Rosie is skilled at tuning in and being able to design interventions that will help increase awareness, as well as equipping people to make significant changes. She has the courage to tell it as she sees it and to do so with empathy and from a sense of possibility. She is also very adaptable to differing client groups and finds the right balance of practice and theory, combined with an ability to inspire."

Mike Jones, Director, Bridge Partnership, United Kingdom

"I made the natural choice to work with N-stinctive: to firstly, bring my team together in a new and profound way; and secondly, because I wanted to take my clients to another level; in terms of what they are experiencing with their leadership and their ability to bring their own teams together.

My first experience of N-stinctive was bringing my team. We don't work together. We are a virtual team scattered around the United Kingdom. We don't get a lot of face time. I wanted something to unify us, bring us together so we could understand each other's strengths. And when I sat down for coffee with Rosie, I appreciated what she was doing and the way she was working and I knew that was the sort of experience I wanted for my team.

We came to the day open, not knowing what to expect. Everyone was very excited because we knew it involved horses, but we did not know what that meant. Rosie and her team led us through an extraordinary impactful programme. Watching my team come together was amazing. We discovered strengths in each other we did not know we had and the way we gelled together in the final exercise was really profound.

For example, speaking to my Events Manager afterwards, she has to host all of our events and deal with all of our clients, up to 300 at the same time, sometimes. When she first started working with us, she was competent, but as yet perhaps, not confident. The confidence level she has gone to since the day has been unbelievable and she always cites her day with N-stinctive as the anchor experience for her really owning her power and being able to delegate and fully manage her career effectively. I am so grateful to Rosie and her team for that. I highly recommend that anyone who wants to being their staff together to tap into the natural talents of their team – which sometimes as the leader you do not see – that this day with Rosie and her horses is an extraordinary experience. You are not going to get anything like it from any other organisation.

There is something unique about the way the horses reflect back – without ego – exactly what energy you bring and exactly how you are gelling. That day cemented us as a team, more than any other leadership or team building course you can ever have. It is second to none. I highly recommend it."

Jo Martin, Women's Leadership Expert and Founder of One of Many

"You really can't learn about Natural Intelligence in a classroom and when I heard about the N-stinctive leadership programme I was intrigued. It is very different to the usual courses. It is held outdoors, working with horses and it took me completely out of my comfort zone, which was exactly what I was doing in my career at the time. The day got me thinking outside the box. I have always thought I was a creative person with the ability to have the confidence and belief that whatever you think you can do, you can and succeed at it.

It was a fun day, but emotionally taxing as well, and what surprised me was the amount of emotional energy I had to build up to work with the live animals. This new way of leading gave me the confidence to know that I was able to manage my new role; to go into the unknown and be successful. I only had four weeks to prove myself, but this day gave me the courage to go to South Africa and prove that I could do it.

Each person in a team is different and this course handled everyone differently, based on each individual. This made us feel at ease and got the best out of us because Rosie took us each out of our respective comfort zones. With players who have been in the game a long time – I have been in it more than 25 years now – you know the game inside out and you know your own expertise inside out, but what you don't know is your team. On this course, we learnt so much about ourselves, but also about the people we work with and about our own, as well as their strengths and weaknesses. Watching the people you work with doing the exercises and how they dealt with each situation was very powerful for us all. Also, it gives each person a sense of identity and it shows them their innate capabilities and that you can use your own Natural Intelligence and push through, taking that into the workforce to be yourself and to succeed at whatever you do.

The three key aspects that really came out of the day with N-stinctive for my team was the confidence and belief to go out and achieve anything we wanted to. And it totally connects you with your work colleagues. Once you really know yourself, you can move on to other people too and you can really see and feel how they operate. It takes a while to understand our own individual Natural Intelligence, but working with N-stinctive reconnects you with doing what you feel is right and believing in it; the absolute key to a successful team.

You are put under pressure to achieve your goals out there with the horses because you have to do it and especially because you have your team watching you. Dealing with the horses makes a huge impact and you can always go back to that belief and see yourself working with the horses. It's like a memorable and practical anchor to take into the future.

The horses have no ego. They don't know about the materialistic aspects of people – where we live and what cars we drive – and working with them strips away all of what you think is important and takes you back to who you really are, the real person. We go to many training presentations, but doing something completely different like this is critical and it gives you and everyone you work with the opportunity to really look at yourself. To question what you are doing and who you are as a person. When you do this with your work team, it is incredibly powerful and that day will remain with us for the rest of our lives."

Mike Catt OBE, former English rugby union rugby player and team coach for the England and Italian teams.

QUOTATION CHAPTER REFERENCES

INTRODUCTION

Maya Flugelon, born Marguerite Annie Johnson, 1928–2014, American poet, singer, memoirist and civil rights activist

CHAPTER 1

Helen Keller, 1880–1968, American author, political activist and lecturer

CHAPTER 2

David Shepherd, 1931–2017, British artist and conservationist

Billy Connolly, Scottish comedian, musician, presenter and actor

Victor Frankl, 1905–1997, Austrian neurologist, psychiatrist, Holocaust survivor and author

The 14th Dalai Lama, Tenzin Gyatso, shortened from Jetsun Jamphel Ngawang Lobsang Yeshe Tenzin Gyatso

Robert Holden, British psychologist, author and broadcaster, known as Britain's foremost expert on happiness

Sir Kenneth Robinson, British author, speaker and international advisor on education in the art to government

David Whyte, English poet, author, speaker and

organisational thinker

CHAPTER 3

Dr Herbert T Benson, American medical doctor and pioneer in mind body medicine

Simon Cohen, British entrepreneur, speaker, broadcaster and communications expert

Martin Raymond, The Future Laboratory, international British speaker and one of the world's leading futurists

Brandon W Johnson, American speaker, author, leadership trainer and organizational development consultant, known as 'the positive energy guy'

CHAPTER 4

Robert Holden, British psychologist, author and broadcaster, known as Britain's foremost expert on happiness

Sir Kenneth Robinson, British author, speaker and international advisor on education in the art to government

CHAPTER 5

Stephen R Covey, 1932–2012, American educator, author, businessman and keynote speaker

The 14th Dalai Lama, Tenzin Gyatso, shortened from Jetsun Jamphel Ngawang Lobsang Yeshe Tenzin Gyatso

Bill Treasurer, entrepreneur's organisational speaker, author, founder and CEO Giant Leap Consulting

The 14th Dalai Lama, Tenzin Gyatso, shortened from Jetsun Jamphel Ngawang Lobsang Yeshe Tenzin Gyatso

Dario Fo, recipient of the 1997 Nobel Prize in Literature. His play, *Accidental Death of an Anarchist* is a classic of 20th century theatre, performed around the world and in more than 40 countries

CHAPTER 6

Stuart Rose Chairman, Marks & Spencers, global retail chain

Dr Rachel Naomi Remen, American author and teacher of alternative medicine

CHAPTER 7

Buckminster Fuller, 1895–1983, American architect, systems theorist, author, designer and inventor

CHAPTER 8

Issac Getz, author and Professor of Leadership and Innovation

Rudyard Kipling, 1865–1936, British journalist, storyteller, writer, poet and novelist

CHAPTER 9

Dr Zeus, pen name of author Theodor Geisel, known for *The Cat in the Hat* series

Dr Wayne Dyer, American philosopher, known as 'the father of motivation'

CHAPTER 10

Lissa Pohl, Head of Leadership, Kentucky University, United States of America

Aristotle, 384–322 BC, an ancient philsopher and scientist born in the city of Stagira, Chalkidiki, in the north of Classical Greece

Caesar Milan, a Mexican-American dog behaviourist

Dr Dawna Markova, co-founder and CEO Emeritus, Professional Thinking Partnership

SUGGESTED FURTHER READING

Robin Wall Kimmerer – *Braiding Sweetgrass: Indigenous Wisdom, Scientific Knowledge and the Teachings of Plants*, 2016

Jordan B Peterson – *12 Rules for Life: An Antidote to Chaos*, 2019

Dr Steve Peters – *The Chimp Paradox: The Mind Management Programme to Help You Achieve Success, Confidence and Happiness*, 2012

Carmine Gallo – *The Storyteller Secret: How TED Speakers and Inspirational Leaders Turn Their Passion into Performance*, 2018

Parker J Palmer – *On the Brink of Everything: Grace, Gravity, and Getting Old*, 2018

Deborah Rowland – *Still Moving: How to Lead Mindful Change*, 2017

Caroline Elton – *Also Human: The Inner Lives of Doctors*, 2018

Wendy Mitchell – *Somebody I Used to Know*, 2019

Mark Rowlands – *The Philosopher and the Wolf: Lessons from the Wild on Love, Death and Happiness*, 2009

Susanna Forrest – *The Age of the Horse: An Equine Journey through Human History*, 2017

Tara Westover – *Educated*, 2018

Linda Kohanov – *The Five Roles of a Master Herder: A*

Revolutionary Model for Socially Intelligent Leadership, 2017

Thomas Moore – *Dark Nights of the Soul: A guide to finding your way through life's ordeals*, 2012

David Abram – *The Spell of the Sensuous: Perception and Language in a More-Than-Human World*, 1997

Chris Barez-Brown – *Wake Up!: Escaping a Life on Autopilot: Escaping Autopilot Life*, 2016

Ken Robinson – *The Element: How Finding Your Passion Changes Everything*, 2010

Alan Hollinghurst – *The Line of Beauty*, 2005

Matthew Syed – *The Greatest: What Sport Teaches Us About Achieving Success*, 2017

Robert Sheldrake – *A New Science of Life*, 2009

Richard Carlson and Joseph Bailey – *Slowing Down to the Speed of Life: How to Create a More Peaceful, Simpler Life from the Inside Out*, 1998

Paulo Coelho – *The Alchemist: A Fable About Following Your Dream*, 2012

Richard Branson – *Screw Business as Usual*, 2013

James Kerr – *Legacy: What the All Blacks can teach us about the business of life*, 2013

Andrew B Morris – *Business to Go: Simple Ideas to Takeaway*, 2012

Matthew Syed – *Blackbox Thinking: Marginal Gains and the Secrets of High Performance – The Surprising Truth About*

Success, 2016

Jennifer Garvey Berger – *Changing on the Job: Developing Leaders for a Complex World*, 2011

Ben Renshaw – *Together, But Something is Missing: How to create and sustain successful relationships*, 2001

Caesar Milan – *Caesar's Way: The Natural, Everyday Guide to Understanding and Correcting Common Dog Problems*, 2008

Rosamund Young – *The Secret Life of Cows*, 2018

Patrick Lencioni – *The Five Dysfunctions of a Team: A Leadership Fable*, 2002

Margaret J Wheatley – *Who Do We Choose To Be?: Facing Reality, Claiming Leadership*, 2017

Yuval Noah Harari – *Sapiens: A Brief History of Humankind*, 2015

Simon Sinek – *Start With Why: How Great Leaders Inspire Everyone To Take Action Paperback*, 2011

Harriet Evans – *The Wildflowers*, 2018

Stephen R Covey – *The Seven Habits of Highly Effective People*, 1999

Robert Holden – *Success Intelligence*, 2010

Annette Simmons – *Quantum Skills for Coaches: A Handbook for Working with Energy and the Body-mind in Coaching*, 2009

Dr Alan Watkins – *Coherence: The Secret Science of Brilliant Leadership*, 2013

Richard Hytner – *Consiglieri: Leading from the Shadows*, 2019

Tom Rath & Barry Conchie – *Strengths-based Leadership: A Landmark Study of Great Leaders, Teams, and the Reasons Why We Follow: Great Leaders, Teams, and Why People Follow*, 2016

Lawrence Anthony (with Graham Spence) – *The Elephant Whisperer: Learning About Life, Loyalty and Freedom From a Remarkable Herd of Elephants*, 2017

Elaine Harrison – *Today is the Day You Change Your Life*, 2011

Maya Angelou – *I Know Why the Caged Bird Sings*, 1984

Queen Noor – *Leap of faith: Memoir of an Unexpected Life*, 2004

Oprah Winfrey – *What I Know For Sure*, 2014

Karen Pryor – *Don't Shoot the Dog: The New Art of Teaching and Training*, 2006

Peter Wohlleben – *The Inner Life of Animals: Surprising Observations of a Hidden World*, 2018

Marianne Williamson – *A Return to Love: Reflections on the Principles of a "Course in Miracles"*, 2015

Janet Street-Porter – *Life's Too F***ing Short*, 2009

Harville Hendrix – *Getting the Love You Want*, 2019

Joan Chittister – *Two Dogs and a Parrot: What Our Animal Friends Can Teach Us About Life*, 2016

Brené Brown – *Braving the Wilderness: The quest for true*

belonging and the courage to stand alone, 2017

Oliver James – *Affluenza*, 2007

Alison Winch – *The Spirit of Natural Leadership: How to Inspire Trust, Respect and a Sense of Shared Purpose*, 2005

Wendy Palmer – *Intuitive Body: Discovering the Wisdom of Conscious Embodiment and Aikido*, 2008

Wendy Palmer & Janet Crawford – *Leadership Embodiment: How the Way We Sit and Stand Can Change the Way We Think and Speak*, 2013

Diana L Guerrero – *What Animals Can Teach Us About Spirituality: Inspiring Lessons from Wild and Tame Creatures*, 2004

Steven Simpson & Dan Miller – *The Processing Pinnacle: An Educator's Guide To Better Processing*, 2006

John Browne – *Connect: How companies succeed by engaging radically with society*, 2016

Margaret Heffernan – *Wilful Blindness: Why We Ignore the Obvious*, 2012

Linda Kohanov – *The Tao of Equus: A Woman's Journey of Healing and Transformation Through the Way of the Horse*, 2007

INDEX

Urbane
BUSINESS

Urbane Publications is dedicated to
developing author voices and publishing business
titles that challenge, educate and inspire.
From trade business titles to innovative
reference books, our goal is to publish what
YOU want to read.
Find out more at
urbanepublications.com